# Introduction to Symbol Crochet

In this book of doilies, we've included not only the traditional crochet instructions, completely written out the way you're used to seeing them, but also the same exact instructions presented in symbols.

In symbol crochet, each stitch is represented by a little picture, or symbol. When symbols are arranged to form a "picture" of the work to be done, it is called a "diagram." The diagram looks quite similar to the finished crocheted piece and shows at a glance just how it is constructed. Each of these seven doilies includes a symbol diagram and stitch key, along with written instructions.

On circular designs such as doilies, the diagram is followed starting at the center, working from right to left (counterclockwise) if you are right-handed, and from left to right (clockwise) if you are left-handed.

The symbol for chain shown in the center ring shows the number of chains needed to get started.

The symbol for slip stitch indicates joining in a ring.

The number of the round is indicated at the beginning of the round.

So sit down and explore this crochet experience called symbol crochet.

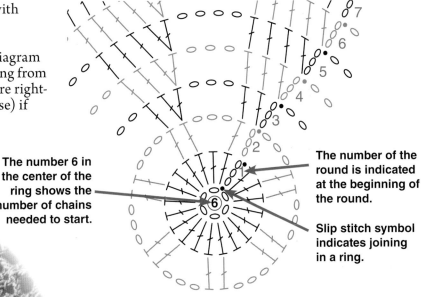

The number 6 in the center of the ring shows the number of chains needed to start.

The number of the round is indicated at the beginning of the round.

Slip stitch symbol indicates joining in a ring.

| STITCH KEY | |
| --- | --- |
| ◦ | Chain (ch) |
| + | Single crochet (sc) |
| • | Slip stitch (sl st) |
| ╆ | Double crochet (dc) |
| ⋀ | Double crochet decrease (dc dec) |
| ⋀ | Beginning cluster (beg cl) |
| ⋀ | Cluster (cl) |
| ⦙ | Beginning 3-double crochet cluster (beg 3-dc cl) |
| ⦙ | 3-double crochet cluster (3-dc cl) |

# Forget-Me-Not

DESIGN BY **AGNES RUSSELL**

## SKILL LEVEL

INTERMEDIATE

## FINISHED SIZE
17 inches in diameter

## MATERIALS
- Size 10 crochet cotton:
  325 yds white
  65 yds aqua
  20 yds yellow
- Size 8/1.50mm steel crochet hook or size needed to obtain gauge
- Plastic-wrap–covered pinning board
- Rustproof straight pins
- Spray starch

## GAUGE
Rnds 1 and 2 = 1½ inches in diameter

Take time to check gauge.

## PATTERN NOTES
Join rounds with a slip stitch as indicated unless otherwise stated.

Chain-3 at beginning of row or round counts as first double crochet unless otherwise stated.

## SPECIAL STITCHES
**Beginning 3-double crochet cluster (beg 3-dc cl):** Ch 3 (see Pattern Notes), keeping last lp of each st on hook, work 2 dc in indicated st, yo, draw through all lps on hook.

**3-double crochet cluster (3-dc cl):** Keeping last lp of each st on hook, 3 dc in indicated st, yo, draw through all lps on hook.

**Beginning shell (beg shell):** (Beg 3-dc cl, ch 3, 3-dc cl) in indicated st or sp.

**Shell:** (3-dc cl, ch 3, 3-dc cl) in indicated st or sp.

**Double shell:** ({3-dc cl, ch 3} twice, 3-dc cl) in indicated st or sp.

**Beginning double shell (beg double shell):** (Beg 3-dc cl, {ch 3, 3-dc cl} twice) in indicated st or sp.

**Cluster decrease (cl dec):** Keeping last lp of each st on hook, work 3 dc in ch sp of current shell and in ch sp of next shell, yo, draw through all lps on hook.

**Shell decrease (shell dec):** 3-dc cl in ch sp of next shell, ch 3, **cl dec** (see Special Stitches), ch 3, 3-dc cl in ch sp of same shell as 2nd part of cl dec.

## CENTER
**Rnd 1 (RS):** With white, ch 8, **join** (see Pattern Notes) in 8th ch from hook to form ring, **beg 3-dc cl** (see Special Stitches) in ring, ch 3, [**3-dc cl** (see Special Stitches) in ring, ch 3] 7 times, join in 3rd ch of beg ch-3. (8 cls, 8 ch-3 sps)

**Rnd 2:** (Sl st, **beg shell**—see Special Stitches—in first ch-3 sp, ch 3, [**shell** (see Special Stitches) in next ch-3 sp, ch 3] around, join in 3rd ch of beg ch-3. (16 cls, 16 ch-3 sps)

**Rnd 3:** (Sl st, ch 1, sc) in next ch-3 sp, ch 4, [sc in next ch-3 sp, ch 4] around, join in first sc. (16 ch-4 sps)

**Rnd 4:** (Sl st, beg shell) in first ch-4 sp, ch 1, [shell in next ch-4 sp, ch 1] around, join in 3rd ch of beg ch-3. *(16 shells)*

**Rnd 5:** (Sl st, beg shell) in ch-3 sp of first shell, ch 4, [shell in ch-3 sp of next shell, ch 4] around, join in 3rd ch of beg ch-3.

**Rnd 6:** (Sl st, beg shell) in ch-3 sp of first shell, ch 4, sl st in next ch-4 sp, ch 4, [shell in ch-3 sp of next shell, ch 4, sl st in next ch-4 sp, ch 4] around, join in 3rd ch of beg ch-3.

**Rnd 7:** (Sl st, beg shell) in ch-3 sp of first shell, ch 9, [shell in ch-3 sp of next shell, ch 9] around, join in 3rd ch of beg ch-3.

**Rnd 8:** (Sl st, beg shell) in ch-3 sp of first shell, ch 4, sc in next ch-9 sp, ch 4, [shell in ch-3 sp of next shell, ch 4, sc in next ch-9 sp, ch 4] around, join in 3rd ch of beg ch-3.

**Rnd 9:** (Sl st, beg shell) in ch-3 sp of first shell, ch 4, (sc, ch 3, sc) in next sc, ch 4, [shell in ch-3 sp of next shell, ch 4, (sc, ch 3, sc) in next sc, ch 4] around, join.

**Rnd 10:** (Sl st, beg shell) in ch-3 sp of first shell, ch 11, [shell in ch-3 sp of next shell, ch 11] around, join in 3rd ch of beg ch-3.

**Rnd 11:** (Sl st, beg shell) in ch-3 sp of first shell, ch 5, sc in next ch-11 sp, ch 5, [shell in ch-3 sp of next shell, ch 5, sc in next ch-11 sp, ch 5] around, join in 3rd ch of beg ch-3.

**Rnd 12:** (Sl st, beg shell) in ch-3 sp of first shell, ch 6, (sc, ch 3, sc) in next sc, ch 6, [shell in ch-3 sp of next shell, ch 6, (sc, ch 3, sc) in next sc, ch 6] around, join in 3rd ch of beg ch-3.

**Rnd 13:** (Sl st, beg shell) in ch-3 sp of first shell, ch 15, [shell in ch-3 sp of next shell, ch 15] around, join in 3rd ch of beg ch-3.

**Rnd 14:** (Sl st, beg shell) in ch-3 sp of first shell, ch 7, sc in next ch-15 sp, ch 7, [shell in ch-3 sp of next shell, ch 7, sc in next ch-15 sp, ch 7] around, join in 3rd ch of beg ch-3.

**Rnd 15:** (Sl st, beg shell) in ch-3 sp of first shell, ch 7, (sc, ch 5, sc) in next sc, ch 7, [shell in ch-3 sp of next shell, ch 7, (sc, ch 5, sc) in next sc, ch 7] around, join in 3rd ch of beg ch-3.

**Rnd 16:** (Sl st, **beg double shell**—*see Special Stitches*—in ch-3 sp of first shell, ch 5, ({sc, ch 3} 3 times, sc) in next ch-5 sp, ch 5, [**double shell** *(see Special Stitches)* in ch-3 sp of next shell, ch 5, ({sc, ch 3} 3 times, sc) in next ch-5 sp, ch 5] around, join in 3rd ch of beg ch-3.

**Rnd 17:** (Sl st, beg shell) in first ch-3 sp, ch 3, shell in next ch-3 sp, ch 3, {3-dc cl in next ch-3 sp, ch 3} 3 times, [{shell in next ch-3 sp, ch 3} twice, {3-dc cl in next ch-3 sp, ch 3} 3 times] around, join in 3rd ch of beg ch-3.

**Rnd 18:** (Sl st, beg shell) in ch-3 sp of first shell, ch 5, shell in ch-3 sp of next shell, ch 3, sk next ch-3 sp, {3-dc cl in next ch-3 sp, ch 3} twice, [shell in ch-3 sp of next shell, ch 5, shell in ch-3 sp of next shell, ch 3, sk next ch-3 sp, {3-dc cl in next ch-3 sp, ch 3} twice] around, join in 3rd ch of beg ch-3.

**Rnd 19:** (Sl st, beg shell) in ch-3 sp of first shell, ch 5, (sc, ch 5, sc) in next ch-5 sp, ch 5, shell in ch-3 sp of next shell, ch 3, sk next ch-3 sp, 3-dc cl in next ch-3 sp, ch 3, [shell in ch-3 sp of next shell, ch 5, (sc, ch 5, sc) in next ch-5 sp, ch 5, shell in ch-3 sp of next shell, ch 3, sk next ch-3 sp, 3-dc cl in next ch-3 sp, ch 3] around, join in 3rd ch of beg ch-3.

**Rnd 20:** (Sl st, beg shell) in ch-3 sp of first shell, ch 5, sk next ch-5 sp, (tr, {ch 1, tr} 4 times) in next ch-5 sp, ch 5, shell in ch-3 sp of next shell, ch 3, sl st in top of next 3-dc cl, ch 3, [shell in ch-3 sp of next shell, ch 5, sk next ch-5 sp, (tr, {ch 1, tr} 4 times) in next ch-5 sp, ch 5, shell in ch-3 sp of next shell, ch 3, sl st in top of next 3-dc cl, ch 3] around, join in 3rd ch of beg ch-3.

**Rnd 21:** (Sl st, beg 3-dc cl) in ch-3 sp of first shell, *ch 5, 3-dc cl in next ch-1 sp, [ch 3, 3-dc cl in next ch-1 sp] 3 times, ch 5**, **shell dec** *(see Special Stitches)*, rep from * around, ending last rep at **, 3-dc cl in ch-3 sp of next shell, ch 3, **cl dec** *(see Special Stitches)*, ch 3, join in top of beg 3-dc cl. Fasten off.

### FIRST FLOWER CENTER
**Row 1 (RS):** Join yellow in first ch-3 sp to the left of any ch-5 sp on rnd 21, *ch 4 *(counts as first dc, ch-1)*, ({dc, ch 1} 4 times, ch 3, sl st) in same ch-3 sp as beg ch-4**, sl st in next ch-3 sp, rep from * twice, ending last rep at **. Fasten off. *(3 groups of 5 ch-1 sps)*

### 2ND–16TH FLOWER CENTERS
**Row 1:** Rep row 1 of First Flower Center.

### FIRST FLOWER PETALS
**Rnd 1 (RS):** Join aqua in first ch sp in any group of 5 ch-1 sps on Flower Center, ch 1, (sc, 3 dc, sc) in each of 5 ch sps, turn *(first petal is now to left)*, join in beg sc. Fasten off.

### REM FLOWER PETALS
**Rnd 1:** Rep rnd 1 of First Flower Petal in each group of 5 ch-1 sps around outer edge. *(16 groups of 3 flowers; total 48 flowers)*

### FINISHING
Adjust flowers so that center flower is on top of the flowers at each side. Pin doily to board in each center ch-3 sp of rnd 21. Saturate with spray starch. Allow to dry completely. ∎

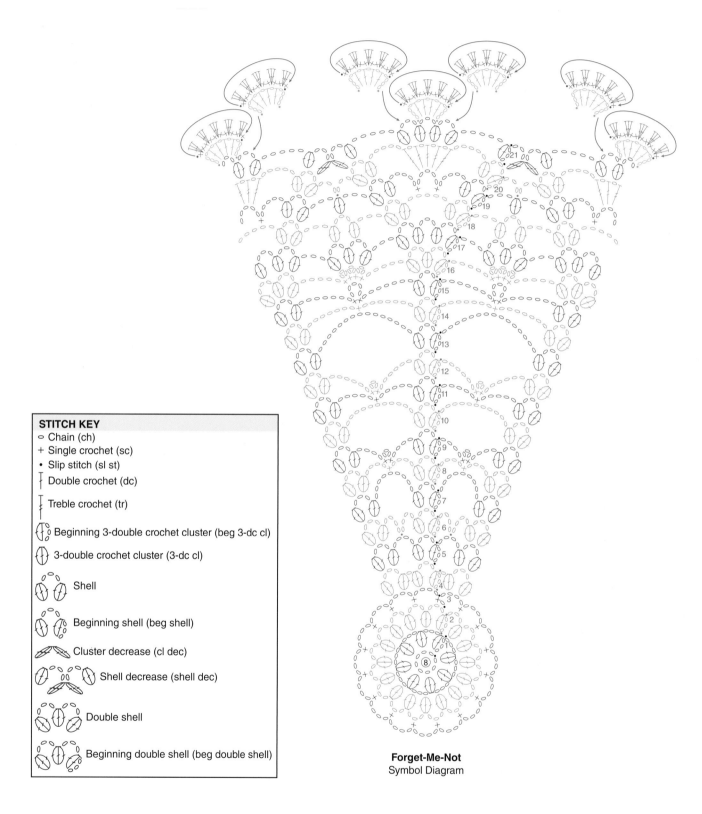

**STITCH KEY**

○ Chain (ch)

+ Single crochet (sc)

• Slip stitch (sl st)

┬ Double crochet (dc)

┬ Treble crochet (tr)

Beginning 3-double crochet cluster (beg 3-dc cl)

3-double crochet cluster (3-dc cl)

Shell

Beginning shell (beg shell)

Cluster decrease (cl dec)

Shell decrease (shell dec)

Double shell

Beginning double shell (beg double shell)

**Forget-Me-Not**
Symbol Diagram

# Harvest **Dance**

DESIGN BY
**KATHRYN WHITE**

## SKILL LEVEL

INTERMEDIATE

## FINISHED SIZE
15½ inches in diameter

## MATERIALS
- Size 20 crochet cotton:
  350 yds cream
- Size 10/1.15mm steel crochet hook
  or size needed to obtain gauge
- Stitch marker

## GAUGE
Rnds 1–3 = 1 inch

## SPECIAL STITCHES
**Picot:** Sl st in 3rd ch from hook.

**Inverted picot:** Ch number of chs instructed, remove lp from hook, insert hook in back lp of ch indicated, pick up dropped lp and pull through. This picot should hang down instead of being upright.

**Beginning 3-treble crochet cluster (beg 3-tr cl):** Holding back last lp of each st on hook, ch 3, 2 tr in same st, yo, pull through all lps on hook.

**3-treble crochet cluster (3-tr cl):** Holding back last lp of each st on hook, 3 tr as indicated, yo, pull through all lps on hook.

**Shell:** (5 tr, ch 3, 5 tr) as indicated.

**5-treble crochet cluster (5-tr cl):** Holding back last lp of each st on hook, 5 tr as indicated, yo, pull through all lps on hook.

**2-double treble crochet cluster (2-dtr cl):** Holding back last lp of each st on hook, 2 dtr in same st, yo, pull through all lps on hook.

## DOILY
**Rnd 1:** Ch 5, sl st in first ch to form ring, ch 1, 12 sc in ring, join with sl st in beg sc. *(12 sc)*

**Rnd 2:** Ch 5 *(counts as first tr and ch-2)*, [tr in next st, ch 2] around, join with sl st in 3rd ch of beg ch-5.

**Rnd 3:** Ch 1, sc in first st, *(sc, **dtr**—*see Stitch Guide*, sc) in next ch-2 sp *(this will create a small nub, push nub to front of work)***, sc in next st, rep from * around, ending last rep at **, join with sl st in beg sc.

**Rnd 4:** Ch 3 *(counts as first tr)*, tr in same st, *ch 4, sk next sc, next dtr and next sc**, 2 tr in next sc, rep from * around, ending last rep at **, join with sl st in 3rd ch of beg ch-3.

**Rnd 5:** Ch 8, **picot** *(see Special Stitches)*, ch 2, tr in same st, *ch 1, sk next ch sp, (tr, ch 5, picot, ch 2, tr) in sp between next 2 sts, rep from * around, join with hdc in 3rd ch of beg ch-3.

**Rnd 6:** Ch 11 *(counts as first tr and ch-8)*, [tr in next ch-1 sp, ch 8] around, join with sl st in 3rd ch of beg ch-11. **Note:** *This rnd may seem to be too tight, but will lay flat after rnd 8.*

**Rnd 7:** Ch 1, sc in first st, 9 sc in next ch-8 sp, [sc in next st, 9 sc in next ch-8 sp] around, join with sl st in **back lp** *(see Stitch Guide)* of beg sc. *(120 sc)*

**Rnd 8:** Working in back lps, ch 1, sc in first st, dtr in next st, [sc in next st, dtr in next st] around, join with sl st in back lp of beg sc. *(60 sc, 60 dtr)*

**Rnd 9:** Working in back lps, ch 1, sc in each of first 5 sts, mark first st of this group, *ch 2, sc in each of next 5 sts, ch 4, turn, (tr, ch 2, tr) in ch-2 sp, ch 4, sl st in marked st, ch 1, turn, 5 sc in ch-4 sp, sc in next tr, ch 3, sl st in base of last sc made, (2 sc, ch 2, 2 sc) in next ch-2 sp, sc in next tr, ch 3, sl st in base of last sc made, 5 sc in next ch-4 sp (*arch completed*)**, sc in each of next 5 sts on last rnd, move marker to first st of this group, rep from * around, ending last rep at **, join with sl st in beg sc. Fasten off. Remove marker.

**Rnd 10:** With RS facing, join with sc in ch-2 sp at top of any arch, ch 14, [sc in ch-2 sp of next arch, ch 14] around, join with sl st in beg sc.

**Rnd 11:** Ch 1, sc in first st, *(4 sc, ch 3, sl st in last sc, [4 sc, ch 3] twice, sl st in last sc, 4 sc) in next ch-14 sp**, sc in next st, rep from * around, ending last rep at **, join with sl st in beg sc. Fasten off.

**Rnd 12:** With RS facing, join with sl st in any ch-3 sp, ch 3, 4 tr in same ch sp, *ch 10, **inverted picot** (*see Special Stitches*) in 4th ch from hook, ch 6**, 5 tr in next ch-3 sp, rep from * around, ending last rep at **, join with sl st in 3rd ch of beg ch-3.

**Rnd 13:** Ch 3, tr in same st, *2 tr in next tr, (tr, ch 3, tr) in next tr, 2 tr in each of next 2 tr, ch 6, sc in next ch sp on this side of inverted picot, ch 3, sc in same ch sp on other side of inverted picot, ch 6**, 2 tr in next tr, rep from * around, ending last rep at **, join with sl st in 3rd ch of beg ch-3.

**Rnd 14:** **Beg 3-tr cl** (*see Special Stitches*), *ch 2, **shell** (*see Special Stitches*) in next ch-3 sp, ch 2, sk next 4 tr, **3-tr cl** (*see Special Stitches*) in next tr, ch 2, (tr, ch 3, tr) in ch-3 sp, ch 2**, 3-tr cl in next tr, rep from * around, ending last rep at **, join with sl st in beg 3-tr cl.

**Rnd 15:** Sl st across to first tr of first shell, beg 3-tr cl in first tr, *ch 2, shell in ch sp of shell, ch 2, 3-tr cl in last tr of same shell, ch 3, (tr, ch 3, tr) in next ch-3 sp, ch 3**, 3-tr cl in first tr of next shell, rep from * around, ending last rep at **, join with sl st in beg 3-tr cl.

**Rnd 16:** Sl st across to first tr of first shell, beg 3-tr cl in first tr, *ch 2, shell in ch sp of shell, ch 2, 3-tr cl in last tr of same shell, ch 4, (2 tr, ch 3, 2 tr) in next ch-3 sp, ch 4**, 3-tr cl in first tr of next shell, rep from * around, ending last rep at **, join with sl st in beg 3-tr cl.

**Rnd 17:** Sl st across to first tr of first shell, beg 3-tr cl in first tr, *ch 2, shell in ch sp of shell, ch 2, 3-tr cl in last tr of same shell, ch 4, 5 tr in next ch-3 sp, ch 4**, 3-tr cl in first tr of next shell, rep from * around, ending last rep at **, join with sl st in beg 3-tr cl.

**Rnd 18:** Sl st across to ch sp of first shell, *(sc, ch 5, **5-tr cl**—*see Special Stitches*, ch 5, sl st in top of last st made, ch 5, sc) in ch sp of shell, ch 6, 2 tr in each of next 2 tr, (tr, ch 3, tr) in next tr, 2 tr in each of next 2 tr, ch 6, rep from * around, join with sl st in beg sc. Fasten off.

**Rnd 19:** Join with sc in ch-5 sp at top of any 5-tr cl, ch 3, sc in same ch-5 sp, *ch 9, 3-tr cl in next tr, ch 2, shell in next ch-3 sp, ch 2, sk next 4 tr, 3-tr cl in next tr, ch 9**, (sc, ch 3, sc) in next ch-5 sp, rep from * around, ending last rep at **, join with sl st in beg sc.

**Rnd 20:** Sl st in first ch-3 sp, ch 3, (tr, ch 3, 2 tr) in same ch sp, *ch 5, sc in next ch-9 sp, ch 4, 3-tr cl in first tr of next shell, ch 2, shell in ch sp of same shell, ch 2, 3-tr cl in last tr of same shell, ch 4, sc in next ch-9 sp, ch 5**, (2 tr, ch 3, 2 tr) in next ch-3 sp, rep from * around, ending last rep at **, join with sl st in 3rd ch of beg ch-3.

**Rnd 21:** Sl st in next st and in next ch-3 sp, ch 3, (tr, [ch 3, 2 tr] 3 times) in same ch sp, *ch 7, 3-tr cl in first tr of next shell, ch 2, shell in ch sp of same shell, ch 2, 3-tr cl in last tr of same shell, ch 7**, (2 tr, [ch 3, 2 tr] 3 times) in next ch-3 sp, rep from * around, ending last rep at **, join with sl st in 3rd ch of beg ch-3.

**Rnd 22:** Sl st in next tr and in next ch-3 sp, ch 3, 4 tr in same ch sp, *[ch 3, 5 tr in next ch sp] twice, ch 2, sc in next ch-7 sp, ch 5, 3-tr cl in first tr of next shell, ch 2, shell in ch sp of same shell, ch 2, 3-tr cl in last tr of same shell, ch 5, sc in next ch-7 sp, ch 2**, 5 tr in next ch-3 sp, rep from * around, ending last rep at **, join with sl st in 3rd ch of beg ch-3.

**Rnd 23:** Ch 3, **tr dec** (*see Stitch Guide*) in next 4 tr, ch 5, sl st in last st made, *[ch 8, tr dec in next 5 tr, ch 5, sl st in last st made] twice, ch 9, **2-dtr cl** (*See Special Stitches*) in first tr of next shell, ch 2, (sc, ch 4, 5-tr cl, ch 5, sl st in last st made, ch 4, sc) in ch sp of same shell, ch 2, 2-dtr cl in last tr of same shell, ch 9**, tr dec in next 5 tr, ch 5, sl st in last st made, rep from * around, ending last rep at **, join with sl st in 3rd ch of beg ch-3. Fasten off.

**Rnd 24:** With RS facing, join with sc in any ch-5 sp at top of a center tr dec, ch 20, sk next ch-5 sp, [sc in next ch-5 sp, ch 20, sk next ch-5 sp] around, join with sl st in beg sc.

**Rnd 25:** Ch 1, sc in first st, 23 sc in next ch-20 sp, [sc in next st, 23 sc in next ch-20 sp] around, join with sl st in beg sc. (*576 sc*)

**Rnd 26:** Working in back lps, ch 1, sc in first st, dtr in next st, [sc in next st, dtr in next st] around, join with sl st in beg sc.

**Rnd 27:** Working in back lps, ch 1, sc in each of first 6 sts, mark first st of this group, *ch 2, sc in each of next 6 sts, turn, ch 5, (tr, ch 5, tr) in ch-2 sp, ch 5, sl st in marked st, turn, 5 sc in ch-5 sp, sc in next tr, ch 3, sl st in base of last sc made, (3 sc, [ch 5, sl st in 5th ch from hook] 3 times, 3 sc) in next ch-5 sp, sc in next st, ch 3, sl st in base of last sc made, 5 sc in next ch-5 sp**, sc in each of next 6 sts on last rnd, move marker to first st of this group, rep from * around, ending last rep at **, join with sl st in beg sc. Fasten off. Remove marker. ∎

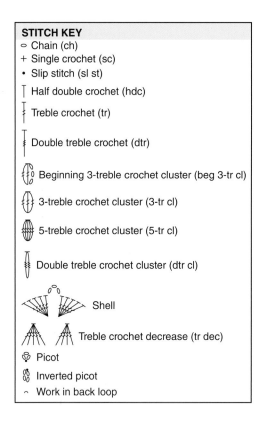

**STITCH KEY**

| | |
|---|---|
| ᵒ | Chain (ch) |
| + | Single crochet (sc) |
| • | Slip stitch (sl st) |
| ⊤ | Half double crochet (hdc) |
| ‡ | Treble crochet (tr) |
| ‡ | Double treble crochet (dtr) |
| | Beginning 3-treble crochet cluster (beg 3-tr cl) |
| | 3-treble crochet cluster (3-tr cl) |
| | 5-treble crochet cluster (5-tr cl) |
| | Double treble crochet cluster (dtr cl) |
| | Shell |
| | Treble crochet decrease (tr dec) |
| | Picot |
| | Inverted picot |
| ‿ | Work in back loop |

**Harvest Dance**
Symbol Diagram

# Square Pineapple

**DESIGN BY**
**JUDY**
**TEAGUE**
**TREECE**

## SKILL LEVEL
■■■□
**INTERMEDIATE**

## FINISHED SIZE
13 inches square

## MATERIALS
- Size 10 crochet cotton:
  350 yds celery
- Size 7/1.65mm steel crochet hook
  or size needed to obtain gauge

**0**
**LACE**

## GAUGE
Rnds 1–4 = 2½ inches across

## PATTERN NOTES
Join with slip stitch as indicated unless otherwise stated.

Chain-4 at beginning of round counts as first treble crochet unless otherwise stated.

## SPECIAL STITCHES
**Cluster (cl):** Yo twice, insert hook in indicated place, yo, pull lp through, [yo, pull through 2 lps on hook] twice, *yo twice, insert hook in same place, yo, pull lp through, [yo, pull through 2 lps on hook] twice, rep from *, yo, pull through all 4 lps on hook.

**Picot:** Ch 3, sl st in top of last st made.

## DOILY
**Rnd 1:** Ch 5, **join** (see Pattern Notes) in beg ch to form ring, **ch 4** (see Pattern Notes), 19 tr in ring, join in 4th ch of beg ch-4. (20 tr)

**Rnd 2:** Ch 4, tr in next st, ch 5, sk next st, sc in next st, ch 5, sk next st, [tr in each of next 2 sts, ch 5, sk next st, sc in next st, ch 5, sk next st] around, join in 4th ch of beg ch-4. (8 tr, 8 ch sps, 4 sc)

**Rnd 3:** Ch 4, tr in next st, *ch 5, sc in next ch sp, ch 3, sc in next ch sp, ch 5**, tr in each of next 2 sts, rep from * around, ending last rep at **, join in 4th ch of beg ch-4. (12 ch sps, 8 tr, 8 sc)

**Rnd 4:** Ch 4, tr in next st, *ch 5, sc in next ch sp, ch 2, (tr, ch 2, tr) in next ch-3 sp, ch 2, sc in next ch sp, ch 5**, tr in each of next 2 sts, rep from * around, ending last rep at **, join in 4th ch of beg ch-4. (16 tr, 12 ch-2 sps, 8 ch-5 sps, 8 sc)

**Rnd 5:** Ch 4, tr in next st, *ch 5, sc in next ch sp, ch 5, sk next ch sp, (sc, ch 5, sc) in next ch sp, ch 5, sk next ch sp, sc in next ch-5 sp, ch 5**, tr in each of next 2 sts, rep from * around, ending last rep at **, join in 4th ch of beg ch-4. (20 ch sps, 16 sc, 8 tr)

**Rnd 6:** Ch 4, tr in next st, *ch 5, sc in next ch sp, ch 3, sc in next ch sp, ch 2, 7 tr in next ch sp, ch 2, sc in next ch sp, ch 3, sc in next ch sp, ch 5**, tr in each of next 2 sts, rep from * around, ending last rep at **, join in 4th ch of beg ch-4. (36 tr, 16 sc, 8 ch-5 sps, 8 ch-3 sps, 8 ch-2 sps)

**Rnd 7:** Ch 4, tr in next st, *[ch 5, sc in next ch sp] twice, ch 3, sk next ch-2 sp, tr in next tr, [ch 1, tr in next st] 6 times, ch 3, sk next ch-2 sp, [sc in next ch sp, ch 5] twice**, tr in each of next 2 sts, rep from * around, ending last rep at **, join in 4th ch of beg ch-4. (36 tr, 24 ch-1 sps)

**Rnd 8:** Ch 4, tr in next st, *[ch 5, sc in next ch sp] twice, ch 4, sk next ch sp, sc in next ch-1 sp, [ch 2, sc in next ch-1 sp] 5 times, ch 4, sk next ch sp, [sc in next ch sp, ch 5] twice**, tr in each of next 2 sts, rep from * around, ending last rep at **, join in 4th ch of beg ch-4. *(40 sc, 8 tr)*

**Rnd 9:** Ch 4, tr in next st, *[ch 5, sc in next ch sp] twice, ch 5, sk next ch sp, sc in next ch-2 sp, [ch 2, sc in next ch-2 sp] 4 times, ch 5, sk next ch sp, [sc in next ch sp, ch 5] twice**, tr in each of next 2 sts, rep from * around, ending last rep at **, join in 4th ch of beg ch-4. *(36 sc, 8 tr)*

**Rnd 10:** Ch 4, tr in next st, *ch 5, sc in next ch sp, ch 3, **cl** *(see Special Stitches)* in next ch sp, ch 6, sk next ch sp, sc in next ch-2 sp, [ch 2, sc in next ch-2 sp] 3 times, ch 6, sk next ch sp, cl in next ch sp, ch 3, sc in next ch sp, ch 5**, tr in each of next 2 sts, rep from * around, ending last rep at **, join in 4th ch of beg ch-4. *(24 sc, 8 cls, 8 tr)*

**Rnd 11:** Ch 4, tr in next st, *ch 5, sc in next ch sp, [ch 5, cl in next ch sp] twice, ch 6, sc in next ch-2 sp, [ch 2, sc in next ch sp] twice, ch 6, [cl in next ch sp, ch 5] twice, sc in next ch sp, ch 5**, tr in each of next 2 sts, rep from * around, ending last rep at **, join in 4th ch of beg ch-4. *(16 cls, 8 tr)*

**Rnd 12:** Ch 4, tr in next st, *ch 5, sc in next ch sp, [ch 5, cl in next ch sp] 3 times, ch 7, sc in next ch-2 sp, ch 2, sc in next ch sp, ch 7, [cl in next ch sp, ch 5] 3 times, sc in next ch sp, ch 5**, tr in each of next 2 sts, rep from * around, ending last rep at **, join in 4th ch of beg ch-4. *(24 cls, 8 tr)*

**Rnd 13:** Ch 4, tr in next st, *ch 5, sc in next ch sp, [ch 5, cl in next ch sp] 4 times, ch 8, sc in next ch-2 sp, ch 8, [cl in next ch sp, ch 5] 4 times, sc in next ch sp, ch 5**, tr in each of next 2 sts, rep from * around, ending last rep at **, join in 4th ch of beg ch-4. *(32 cls, 8 tr)*

**Rnd 14:** Ch 4, tr in next st, *[ch 5, sc in next ch sp] twice, [ch 5, cl in next ch sp] 3 times, ch 5, sc in next ch-8 sp, ch 3, sc in next ch-8 sp, [ch 5, cl in next ch sp] 3 times, [ch 5, sc in next ch sp] twice, ch 5**, tr in each of next 2 sts, rep from * around, ending last rep at **, join in 4th ch of beg ch-4. *(24 cls, 8 tr)*

**Rnd 15:** Ch 4, tr in next st, *[ch 5, sc in next ch sp] 3 times, [ch 5, cl in next ch sp] twice, ch 5, sc in next ch sp, ch 3, cl in next ch sp, ch 3, sc in next ch sp, [ch 5, cl in next ch sp] twice, [ch 5, sc in next ch sp] 3 times, ch 5**, tr in each of next 2 sts, rep from * around, ending last rep at **, join in 4th ch of beg ch-4. *(20 cls, 8 tr)*

**Rnd 16:** Ch 4, tr in next st, *[ch 5, sc in next ch sp] 4 times, ch 5, cl in next ch sp, ch 5, sc in next ch sp, [ch 3, cl in next ch sp] twice, ch 3, sc in next ch sp, ch 5, cl in next ch sp, [ch 5, sc in next ch sp] 4 times, ch 5**, tr in each of next 2 sts, rep from * around, ending last rep at **, join in 4th ch of beg ch-4. *(16 cls, 8 tr)*

**Rnd 17:** Ch 4, tr in next st, *[ch 5, sc in next ch sp] 6 times, [ch 3, cl in next ch sp] 3 times, ch 3, sc in next ch sp, [ch 5, sc in next ch sp] 5 times, ch 5**, tr in each of next 2 sts, rep from * around, ending last rep at **, join in 4th ch of beg ch-4. *(48 ch-5 sps, 12 cls, 8 tr)*

**Rnd 18:** Ch 4, tr in next st, *[ch 5, sc in next ch sp] twice, ch 3, cl in next ch sp, ch 3, sc in next ch sp, ch 5, sc in next ch sp, ch 2, 7 tr in next ch sp, ch 2, sc in next ch sp, [ch 3, cl in next ch sp] twice, ch 3, sc in next ch sp, ch 2, 7 tr in next ch sp, ch 2, sc in next ch sp, ch 5, sc in next ch sp, ch 3, cl in next ch sp, ch 3, sc in next ch sp, ch 5, sc in next ch sp, ch 5**, tr in each of next 2 sts, rep from * around, ending last rep at **, join in 4th ch of beg ch-4. *(64 tr, 16 cls)*

**Rnd 19:** Ch 4, tr in next st, *[ch 5, sc in next ch sp] twice, [ch 3, cl in next ch sp] twice, ch 3, sc in next ch sp, ch 3, sc in next tr, [ch 2, sc in next tr] 6 times, ch 3, sk next ch sp, sc in next ch sp, ch 3, cl in next ch sp, ch 3, sc in next ch sp, ch 3, sc in next tr, [ch 2, sc in next tr] 6 times, ch 3, sk next ch sp, sc in next ch sp, [ch 3, cl in next ch sp] twice, ch 3, [sc in next ch sp, ch 5] twice**, tr in each of next 2 sts, rep from * around, ending last rep at **, join in 4th ch of beg ch-4. *(48 ch-2 sps, 20 cls, 8 tr)*

**Rnd 20:** Ch 4, tr in next st, *[ch 5, sc in next ch sp] twice, [ch 3, cl in next ch sp] 3 times, ch 5, sk next ch sp, sc in next ch-2 sp, [ch 2, sc in next ch-2 sp] 5 times, ch 5, sk next ch sp, sc in next ch sp, ch 5, sc in next ch sp, ch 5, sk next ch sp, sc in next ch-2 sp, [ch 2, sc in next ch-2 sp] 5 times, ch 5, sk next ch sp, [cl in next ch sp, ch 3] 3 times, [sc in next ch sp, ch 5] twice**, tr in each of next 2 sts, rep from * around, ending last rep at **, join in 4th ch of beg ch-4. *(40 ch-2 sps, 24 cls, 8 tr)*

**Rnd 21:** Ch 4, tr in next st, *[ch 5, sc in next ch sp] 3 times, [ch 3, cl in next ch sp] twice, ch 3, sc in next ch sp, ch 4, sc in next ch-2 sp, [ch 2, sc in next ch-2 sp] 4 times, ch 3, sc in next ch sp, ch 3, 7 tr in next ch-5 sp, ch 3, sc in next ch sp, ch 3, sc in next ch-2 sp, [ch 2, sc in next ch-2 sp] 4 times, ch 4, sc in next ch sp, [ch 3, cl in next ch sp] twice, ch 3, sc in next ch sp, [ch 5, sc in next ch sp] twice, ch 5**, tr in each of next 2 sts, rep from * around, ending last rep at **, join in 4th ch of beg ch-4. *(36 tr, 32 ch-2 sps, 16 cls)*

**Rnd 22:** Ch 4, tr in next st, *[ch 5, sc in next ch sp] 4 times, ch 3, cl in next ch sp, [ch 3, sc in next sp] twice, ch 3, sc in next ch-2 sp, [ch 2, sc in next ch-2 sp] 3 times, ch 3, sc in next ch sp, ch 3, sc in next tr, [ch 2, sc in next tr] 6 times, ch 3, sc in next ch sp, ch 3, sc in next ch-2 sp, [ch 2, sc in next ch-2 sp] 3 times, [ch 3, sc in next ch sp] twice, ch 3, cl in next ch sp, ch 3, sc in next ch sp, [ch 5, sc in next ch sp] 3 times, ch 5**, tr in each of next 2 sts, rep from * around, ending last rep at **, join in 4th ch of beg ch-4. *(48 ch-2 sps, 8 cls, 8 tr)*

**Rnd 23:** Ch 4, tr in next st, *[ch 5, sc in next ch sp] 7 times, ch 4, sk next ch sp, sc in next ch-2 sp, [ch 2, sc in next ch-2 sp] twice, ch 4, sk next ch sp, sc in next ch sp, ch 3, sc in next ch-2 sp, [ch 2, sc in next ch-2 sp] 5 times, ch 3, sc in next ch sp, ch 4, sk next ch sp, sc in next ch-2 sp, [ch 2, sc in next ch-2 sp] twice, ch 4, sk next ch sp, sc in next ch sp, [ch 5, sc in next ch sp] 6 times, ch 5**, tr in each of next 2 sts, rep from * around, ending last rep at **, join in 4th ch of beg ch-4. *(56 ch-5 sps, 36 ch-2 sps, 16 ch-4 sps, 8 ch-3 sps, 8 tr)*

**Rnd 24:** Ch 4, tr in next st, *[ch 5, sc in next ch sp] 7 times, ch 6, sk next ch sp, sc in next ch-2 sp, ch 2, sc in next ch sp, ch 6, sk next ch sp, sc in next ch sp, ch 3, sc in next ch-2 sp, [ch 2, sc in next ch-2 sp] 4 times, ch 3, sc in next ch sp, ch 6, sk next ch sp, sc in next ch-2 sp, ch 2, sc in next ch-2 sp, ch 6, sk next ch sp, sc in next ch sp, [ch 5, sc in next ch sp] 6 times, ch 5**, tr in each of next 2 sts, rep from * around, ending last rep at **, join in 4th ch of beg ch-4. *(56 ch-5 sps, 24 ch-2 sps, 16 ch-6 sps, 8 tr)*

**Rnd 25:** Ch 4, tr in next st, *[ch 5, sc in next ch sp] 7 times, ch 7, sk next ch sp, sc in next ch-2 sp, ch 7, sk next ch sp, sc in next ch sp, ch 3, sc in next ch-2 sp, [ch 2, sc in next ch-2 sp] 3 times, ch 3, sc in next ch sp, ch 7, sk next ch sp, sc in next ch-2 sp, ch 7, sk next ch sp, sc in next ch sp, [ch 5, sc in next ch sp] 6 times, ch 5**, tr in each of next 2 sts, rep from * around, ending last rep at **, join in 4th ch of beg ch-4. *(56 ch-5 sps, 16 ch-7 sps, 8 tr)*

**Rnd 26:** Ch 4, tr in next st, *[ch 5, sc in next ch sp] 10 times, ch 4, sc in next ch-2 sp, [ch 2, sc in next ch-2 sp] twice, ch 4, sc in next ch sp, [ch 5, sc in next ch sp] 9 times, ch 5**, tr in each of next 2 sts, rep from * around, ending last rep at **, join in 4th ch of beg ch-4. *(80 ch-5 sps, 8 ch-4 sps, 8 tr)*

**Rnd 27:** Ch 4, tr in next st, *[ch 5, sc in next ch sp] 11 times, ch 5, sc in next ch-2 sp, ch 2, sc in next ch-2 sp, [ch 5, sc in next ch sp] 11 times, ch 5**, tr in each of next 2 sts, rep from * around, ending last rep at **, join in 4th ch of beg ch-4. *(96 ch-5 sps, 8 tr)*

**Rnd 28:** Ch 4, tr in next st, *[ch 5, sc in next ch sp] 12 times, ch 5, sk next ch-2 sp, sc in next ch sp, [ch 5, sc in next ch sp] 11 times, ch 5**, tr in each of next 2 sts, rep from * around, ending last rep at **, join in 4th ch of beg ch-4. *(100 ch-5 sps, 8 tr)*

**Rnd 29:** Ch 1, sc in first st, **picot** *(see Special Stitches)*, sc in next st, ch 4, (sc, picot, sc, ch 4) in each ch sp across to next tr, *sc in next tr, picot, sc in next tr, ch 4, (sc, picot, sc, ch 4) in each ch sp across to next tr, rep from * around, join in 4th ch of beg ch-7. Fasten off. ■

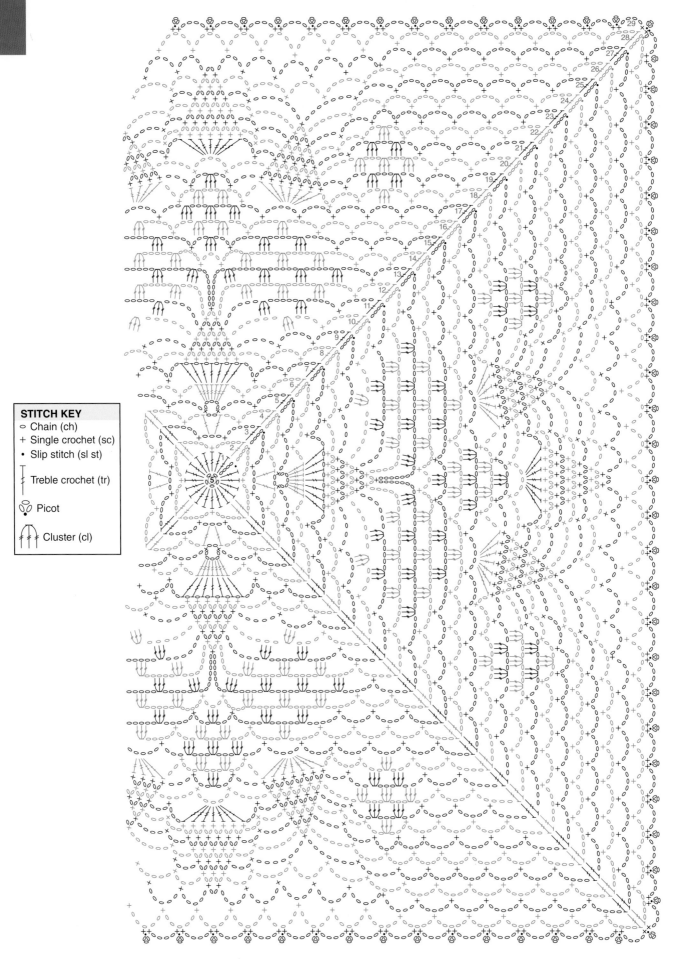

**STITCH KEY**
○ Chain (ch)
+ Single crochet (sc)
• Slip stitch (sl st)
╪ Treble crochet (tr)
♡ Picot
⋔ Cluster (cl)

**Square Pineapple**
Symbol Diagram

# Rose Garden

DESIGN BY
**KATHRYN WHITE**

## SKILL LEVEL

INTERMEDIATE

## FINISHED SIZE
13 inches in diameter

## MATERIALS
- Aunt Lydia's Classic Crochet size 10 crochet cotton (solids: 350 yds per ball; shaded: 300 yds per ball): 1 ball each #419 ecru, #26 shaded purples, #15 shaded pinks and #180 dark shaded yellows
- DMC Color Variations 6-strand embroidery floss: 4 skeins #4050
- Size 7/1.65mm steel crochet hook or size needed to obtain gauge
- Size H/8/5mm crochet hook

## GAUGE
Rose = 1½ inches in diameter

## PATTERN NOTES
Use size 7 steel hook unless otherwise stated.

Embroidery floss is worked with 4 strands held together.

## SPECIAL STITCHES
**Padded ring:** Using size H hook, loosely wrap thread 8 to 10 times around end opposite the hook. Gently slide lps off and insert size 7 steel hook with your working thread in ring, pull lp through, ch 1 and sc in ring. Do not wrap it too tightly or you will have trouble sliding it off the hook and retaining its shape.

**Picot loop (picot lp):** [Ch 5, sl st in 4th ch from hook] twice.

**Beginning shell (beg shell):** Ch 2 (*counts as first dc*), (dc, ch 3, 2 dc) in same ch sp.

**Shell:** (2 dc, ch 3, 2 dc) as indicated.

**Picot:** Ch 4, sl st in 4th ch from hook.

## CENTER ROSE
**Rnd 1:** With shaded purples, work **padded ring** (*see Special Stitches*) with 10 wraps, 17 sc in ring, join with sl st in beg sc. (*18 sc*)

**Rnd 2:** Ch 1, sc in first sc, ch 3, sk next 2 sc, [sc in next sc, ch 3, sk next 2 sc] around, join with sl st in beg sc. (*6 ch sps*)

**Rnd 3:** Sl st in first ch sp, ch 1, (sc, 5 dc, sc) in same ch sp and in each ch sp around, join with sl st in beg sc. (*6 petals*)

**Rnd 4:** Working behind petals, ch 1, sc in first sc of rnd 2, ch 4, [sc in next sc of rnd 2, ch 4] around, join with sl st in beg sc.

**Rnd 5:** Sl st in next ch sp, ch 1, (sc, 7 dc, sc) in same ch sp and in each ch sp around, join with sl st in beg sc. (*6 petals*)

**Rnd 6:** Working behind petals, ch 1, sc in first sc of rnd 4, ch 5, [sc in next sc of rnd 4, ch 5] around, join with sl st in beg sc.

**Rnd 7:** Sl st in first ch sp, ch 1, (sc, 9 dc, sc) in same ch sp and in each ch sp around, join with sl st in beg sc. Fasten off. (*6 petals*)

## DOILY BODY

**Rnd 1:** With 4 strands of embroidery floss held tog, join with sl st in sp between any 2 petals, ch 8 (*counts as 1 dc and 6 ch*), sc in 5th dc of next petal, *ch 6, dc in sp between petals, ch 6, sc in 5th dc of next petal, rep from * around, join with ch 2, dc in 2nd ch of beg ch-8, forming last ch sp.

**Rnd 2:** Ch 1, sc in last sp made, **picot lp** (*see Special Stitches*), ch 2, *sc in next ch sp, picot lp, ch 2, rep from * around, join with sl st in beg sc.

**Rnd 3:** Sl st across to sp between picots on first picot lp, ch 1, sc in same sp, picot lp, ch 2, [sc in sp between picots on next picot lp, picot lp, ch 2] around, join with sl st in beg sc.

**Rnd 4:** Sl st across to sp between picots on first picot lp, ch 1, sc in same sp, *ch 6, sl st in 4th ch from hook, ch 5, sl st in 4th ch from hook, ch 3**, sc in sp between next 2 picots, rep from * around, ending last rep at **, join with sl st in beg sc. Fasten off.

**Rnd 5:** With RS facing, join ecru with sl st in sp between any 2 picots, ch 5 (*counts as first dc and ch-3*), dc in same sp, ch 8, *(dc, ch 2, dc) in sp between next 2 picots, ch 8, rep from * around, join with sl st in 2nd ch of beg ch-5.

**Rnd 6:** Sl st in first ch sp, **beg shell** (*see Special Stitches*), ch 1, [**shell** (*see Special Stitches*) in next ch sp, ch 1] around, join with sl st in 2nd ch of beg ch-2. (*24 shells*)

**Rnd 7:** Sl st across to first ch sp, sl st in ch sp, beg shell in same ch sp, ch 1, [shell in ch sp of next shell, ch 1] around, join with sl st in 2nd ch of beg ch-2.

**Rnd 8:** Sl st across to first ch sp, sl st in ch sp, beg shell, *ch 4, (sc, ch 3, sc) in ch sp of next shell, ch 4**, shell in ch sp of next shell, rep from * around, ending last rep at **, join with sl st in 2nd ch of beg ch-2.

**Rnd 9:** Sl st across to first ch sp, sl st in ch sp, ch 2, (2 dc, ch 3, 3 dc) in same ch sp, ch 5, **tr dec** (*see Stitch Guide*) in next 2 ch-4 sps, ch 5**, (3 dc, ch 3, 3 dc) in ch sp of next shell, rep from * around, ending last rep at **, join with sl st in 2nd ch of beg ch-2.

**Rnd 10:** Sl st across to first ch sp, sl st in ch sp, ch 2, (2 dc, ch 4, 3 dc) in same ch sp, *ch 4, (dc, ch 3, dc) in tr dec, ch 4**, (3 dc, ch 4, 3 dc) in next ch-2 sp, rep from * around, ending last rep at **, join with sl st in 2nd ch of beg ch-2.

**Rnd 11:** Sl st across to first ch sp, sl st in ch sp, ch 3 (*counts as first tr*), 14 tr in same ch sp, *ch 2, sk next ch-4 sp, (sc, ch 3, sc) in next ch-3 sp, ch 2, sk next ch-4 sp**, 15 tr in next ch-4 sp, rep from * around, ending last rep at **, join with sl st in 3rd ch of beg ch-3. (*12 tr groups*)

**Rnd 12:** Sl st in next st, ch 3, tr dec in next 3 sts, *[ch 7, tr dec in last st worked in and next 3 sts] 3 times, ch 2**, sk first tr of next tr group, tr dec in next 4 sts, rep from * around, ending last rep at **, join with sl st in 3rd ch of beg ch-3. Fasten off.

## ROSE

**Make 4 each shaded purples, shaded pinks and dark shaded yellows.**
**Rnds 1–6:** Rep rnds 1–6 of Center Rose.

**Rnd 7:** Sl st in first ch sp, ch 1, (sc, 9 dc, sc) in same ch sp and in each of next 2 ch sps, (sc, 5 dc, sl st in rightmost ch-7 sp of any group, 4 dc, sc) in next ch sp of Rose, (sc, 5 dc, sl st in ch-2 sp between groups, 4 dc, sc) in next ch sp of Rose, (sc, 5 dc, sl st in leftmost ch-7 sp of next group, 4 dc, sc) in next ch sp of Rose, join with sl st in beg sc. Fasten off.

Continue making Roses around Doily, alternating colors, until you have 12 Roses attached.

## PADDED FLOWER

**Make 12.**
With ecru, work padded ring, ch 4, 2 sc in ring, ch 2, sl st in center dc of rightmost unjoined petal of Rose, ch 2, 2 sc in padded ring, ch 4, 2 sc in ring, ch 2, sl st in unjoined ch-7 sp on Doily between Roses, ch 2, 2 sc in ring, ch 4, 2 sc in ring, ch 2, sl st in center dc of leftmost unjoined petal of next Rose, ch 2, 2 sc in ring, ch 4, 2 sc in ring, ch 4, sc in ring, join with sl st in beg sc. Fasten off.

*Note: You should have 3 unjoined ch-4 lps at top of each Padded Flower, and 1 unjoined lp between each joined lp, for a total of 8 lps.*

Work Padded Flowers between Roses around.

## CONTINUE DOILY BODY

**Rnd 13:** With RS facing, join ecru with sl st in same dc of Rose as rightmost joining st of any Padded Flower, ch 7 *(counts as first tr and ch-4)*, *sk next unjoined lp on Padded Flower, (dc, ch 3, dc) in next lp, ch 4, sk next unjoined lp, tr in same dc on next Rose as leftmost joining st of same Padded Flower, ch 7, sc in center dc of next unjoined petal, ch 7**, tr in same dc on next petal as rightmost joining st of next Padded Flower, ch 4, rep from * around, ending last rep at **, join with sl st in 3rd ch of beg ch-7.

**Rnd 14:** Ch 1, sc in first st, *ch 4, (dc, {ch 2, 2 tr} twice, ch 2, dc) in next ch-3 sp, ch 4, sk next st, sc in next tr, ch 6, shell in next sc, ch 6**, sc in next tr, rep from * around, ending last rep at **, join with sl st in beg sc. Fasten off.

**Rnd 15:** Join 4 strands embroidery floss with sc in first st, *5 sc in next ch-4 sp, sc in next dc, (sc, **picot**—*see Special Stitches*, sc) in next ch-2 sp, sc in each of next 2 tr, (2 sc, picot, ch 5, sl st in 5th ch from hook, picot, 2 sc) in next ch-2 sp, sc in each of next 2 tr, (sc, picot, sc) in next ch-2 sp, sc in next dc, 5 sc in next ch-4 sp, sc in next sc, 7 sc in next ch-6 sp, sc in next tr, (picot, sc) in next tr, (sc, picot, sc) in next ch sp, sc in next tr, (picot, sc) in next tr, 7 sc in next ch-6 sp**, sc in next sc, rep from * around, ending last rep at **, join with sl st in beg sc. Fasten off. ∎

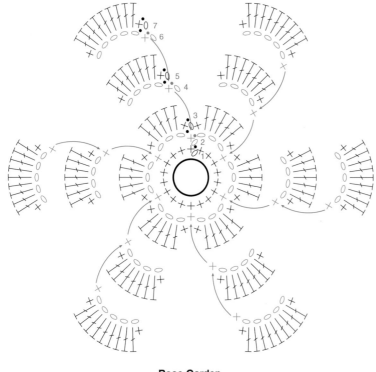

**Rose Garden**
Rose Symbol Diagram

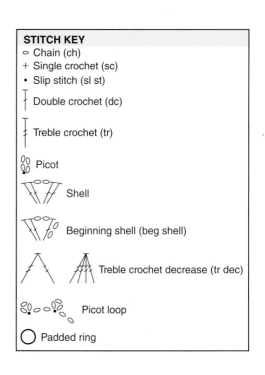

**STITCH KEY**
◦ Chain (ch)
+ Single crochet (sc)
• Slip stitch (sl st)
⊤ Double crochet (dc)
Ŧ Treble crochet (tr)
Picot
Shell
Beginning shell (beg shell)
Treble crochet decrease (tr dec)
Picot loop
◯ Padded ring

**Rose Garden**
Symbol Diagram

# Aquamarine Starcatcher

DESIGN BY **KATHRYN WHITE**

## SKILL LEVEL

INTERMEDIATE

## FINISHED SIZE
16 inches in diameter

## MATERIALS
- Size 10 crochet cotton:
  350 yds aqua
- Size 7/1.65mm steel crochet hook
  or size needed to obtain gauge

## GAUGE
Rnds 1–4 = 2 inches

## SPECIAL STITCHES
**Beginning shell (beg shell):** Ch 2 (*counts as first dc*), (dc, ch 2, 2 dc) as indicated.

**Shell:** (2 dc, ch 2, 2 dc) as indicated.

**3-treble crochet cluster (3-tr cl):** Holding back last lp of each st on hook, 3 tr as indicated, yo, pull through all lps on hook.

**4-treble crochet cluster (4-tr cl):** Holding back last lp of each st on hook, 4 tr as indicated, yo, pull through all lps on hook.

**Picot:** Ch 5, sl st in 4th ch from hook, ch 2.

**Chain-4 picot (ch-4 picot):** Ch 4, sl st in 4th ch from hook.

## DOILY
**Rnd 1:** Ch 5, sl st in first ch to form ring, ch 1, 16 sc in ring, join with sl st in beg sc. (*16 sc*)

**Rnd 2:** Ch 1, sc in first st, [ch 3, sk next st, sc] around, join with ch 1, hdc in beg sc forming last sp. (*8 ch sps*)

**Rnd 3:** Ch 1, sc in sp just made, [ch 4, sc in next ch sp] around, join with ch 1, dc in beg sc forming last sp.

**Rnd 4:** **Beg shell** (*see Special Stitches*) in sp just made, ch 1, [**shell** (*see Special Stitches*) in next ch sp, ch 1] around, join with sl st in 2nd ch of beg ch-2. (*8 shells*)

**Rnd 5:** Sl st across to first ch-2 sp, beg shell, [ch 5, shell in next ch-2 sp] around, join with ch 1, tr in 2nd ch of beg ch-2 forming last ch sp.

**Rnd 6:** Ch 4 (*counts as first dc and ch-2*), dc in same sp, ch 4, *(sc, ch 3, sc) in next ch-2 sp, ch 4**, (dc, ch 2, dc) in next ch-5 sp, ch 4, rep from * around, ending last rep at **, join with sl st in 2nd ch of beg ch-4.

**Rnd 7:** Sl st in first ch-2 sp, ch 3 (*counts as first tr*), (2 tr, ch 3, 3 tr) in same ch sp, ch 9, [(3 tr, ch 3, 3 tr) in next ch sp, ch 9] around, join with sl st in 3rd ch of beg ch-3.

**Rnd 8:** Ch 1, [sc in each st and each ch across to next ch-9 sp, ch 10, sk ch-9 sp] around, join with sl st in beg sc.

**Rnd 9:** Ch 3, **tr dec** (*see Stitch Guide*) in next 2 sts, *ch 4, sk next st, sc in next st, ch 4, sk next st, tr dec in next 3 sts, ch 4, working over ch-10 sp on last rnd, (dc, ch 2, dc) in ch-9 sp on rnd before last, ch 4**, tr dec in next 3 sts, rep from * around, ending last rep at **, join with sl st in top of first tr dec.

**Rnd 10:** Ch 3, **3-tr cl** (*see Special Stitches*) in same st, *ch 3, tr in each of next 2 ch-4 sps, ch 3, **4-tr cl** (*see Special Stitches*) in next tr dec, ch 4, 5 dc in next ch-2 sp, ch 4**, 4-tr cl in next tr dec, rep from * around, ending last rep at **, join with sl st in top of beg 3-tr cl.

**Rnd 11:** Ch 3, 3-tr cl in same st, *ch 4, 5 tr in sp between next 2 tr, ch 4, 4-tr cl in next 4-tr cl, ch 4, dc dec in next 5 dc, ch 4, sl st in last st made, ch 4**, 4-tr cl in next 4-tr cl, rep from * around, ending last rep at **, join with sl st in beg 3-tr cl.

**Rnd 12:** Ch 3, 3-tr cl in same st, *ch 7, tr dec in next 5 sts, ch 5, sl st in top of tr dec just made, ch 7, 4-tr cl in next 4-tr cl, ch 7**, 4-tr cl in next 4-tr cl, rep from * around, ending last rep at **, join with sl st in beg 3-tr cl.

**Rnd 13:** Ch 3, 3-tr cl in same st, *ch 6, sk next ch-7 sp, 9 tr in next ch-5 sp, ch 6, sk next ch-7 sp, 4-tr cl in next 4-tr cl, ch 5**, 4-tr cl in next 4-tr cl, rep from * around, ending last rep at **, join with sl st in beg 3-tr cl.

**Rnd 14:** Ch 3, 3-tr cl in same st, *ch 5, tr in next st, [ch 1, tr in next st] 8 times, ch 5, 4-tr cl in next 4-tr cl, ch 4**, 4-tr cl in next 4-tr cl, rep from * around, ending last rep at **, join with sl st in beg 3-tr cl.

**Rnd 15:** Ch 3, 3-tr cl in same st, *ch 7, sc in next st, [**picot** (*see Special Stitches*), sk next tr, sc in next tr] 4 times, ch 7, 4-tr cl in next 4-tr cl, ch 3**, 4-tr cl in next 4-tr cl, rep from * around, ending last rep at **, join with sl st in beg 3-tr cl.

**Rnd 16:** Ch 3, 3-tr cl in same st, *ch 12, sk next 2 picots, 5 tr in next sc, ch 12, 4-tr cl in next 4-tr cl, ch 4**, 4-tr cl in next 4-tr cl, rep from * around, ending last rep at **, join with sl st in beg 3-tr cl.

**Rnd 17:** Ch 3, 3-tr cl in same st, *ch 10, tr in next tr, **ch-4 picot** (*see Special Stitches*), tr in same tr as last st, tr in next tr, ch-4 picot, tr in each of next 2 tr, ch-4 picot, tr in next tr, ch-4 picot, tr in same tr as last st, ch 10, 4-tr cl in next 4-tr cl, ch 5, sc in next ch sp, ch 5**, 4-tr cl in next 4-tr cl, rep from * around, ending last rep at **, join with sl st in beg 3-tr cl.

**Rnd 18:** Ch 3, 3-tr cl in same st, *ch 4, working over ch-10 of last rnd, (tr, ch-4 picot, tr) in ch-12 sp on rnd before last, ch 6, sk next 3 tr, 3 tr in next st, ch 6, working over ch-10 of last rnd, (tr, ch-4 picot, tr) in ch-12 sp on rnd before last, ch 4, 4-tr cl in next 4-tr cl, [ch 5, sc in next ch-5 sp] twice, ch 5**, 4-tr cl in next 4-tr cl, rep from * around, ending last rep at **, join with sl st in beg 3-tr cl.

**Rnd 19:** Ch 3, 3-tr cl in same st, *ch 10, sk next 2 ch sps, dc in each of next 3 sts, ch 10, 4-tr cl in next 4-tr cl, [ch 5, sc in next ch sp] 3 times, ch 5**, 4-tr cl in next 4-tr cl, rep from * around, ending last rep at **, join with sl st in beg 3-tr cl.

**Rnd 20:** Ch 3, 3-tr cl in same st, *ch 7, (tr, ch-4 picot, tr) in next tr, tr in next tr, (tr, ch-4 picot, tr) in next tr, ch 7, 4-tr cl in next 4-tr cl, [ch 5, sc in next ch sp] twice, 5 tr in next sc, [sc in next ch sp, ch 5] twice**, 4-tr cl in next 4-tr cl, rep from * around, ending last rep at **, join with sl st in beg 3-tr cl.

**Rnd 21:** Ch 3, 3-tr cl in same st, *ch 7, sk next 2 tr, 4-tr cl in next tr, ch-4 picot, ch 7, 4-tr cl in next 4-tr cl, [ch 5, sc in next ch sp] twice, ch 5, sk next 2 tr, sc in next tr, [ch 5, sc in next ch sp] twice, ch 5**, 4-tr cl in next 4-tr cl, rep from * around, ending last rep at **, join with sl st in beg 3-tr cl.

**Rnd 22:** Ch 3, 3-tr cl in same st, *ch 6, sc in ch-4 picot, ch 6, 4-tr cl in next 4-tr cl, [ch 5, sc in next ch sp] twice, 5 tr in next sc, sc in next ch sp, ch 5, sc in next ch sp, 5 tr in next sc, [sc in next ch sp, ch 5] twice**, 4-tr cl in next 4-tr cl, rep from * around, ending last rep at **, join with sl st in beg 3-tr cl.

**Rnd 23:** Ch 3, 3-tr cl in same st, *ch 6, sc in next st, ch 6, 4-tr cl in next 4-tr cl, [ch 5, sc in next ch sp] twice, ch 5, sk next 2 tr, sc in next tr, ch 5, sc in next ch sp, ch 5, sk next 2 tr, sc in next tr, ch 5, [sc in next ch sp, ch 5] twice**, 4-tr cl in next 4-tr cl, rep from * around, ending last rep at **, join with sl st in beg ch-3 cl.

**Rnd 24:** Ch 3, 3-tr cl in same st, *ch 6, 4-tr cl in next 4-tr cl, [ch 5, sc in next ch sp] 4 times, 5 tr in next sc, [sc in next ch sp, ch 5] 4 times**, 4-tr cl in next 4-tr cl, rep from * around, ending last rep at **, join with sl st in beg 3-tr cl.

**Rnd 25:** Ch 3, 3-tr cl in same st, *ch 1, dc in next ch sp, ch 1, 4-tr cl in next 4-tr cl, [ch 5, sc in next ch sp] 4 times, ch 5, sk next 2 tr, sc in next st, ch 5, [sc in next ch sp, ch 5] 4 times**, 4-tr cl in next 4-tr cl, rep from * around, ending last rep at **, join with sl st in beg 3-tr cl.

**Rnd 26:** Ch 3, holding back last lp of each st on hook, 3 tr in same st and 4 tr in next 4-tr cl, yo, pull through all lps on hook, *ch 7, sl st in top of last st made, ch 7, [sc in next ch sp, ch 5] 9 times, sc in next ch sp, ch 7**, holding back last lp of each st on hook, 4 tr in each of next 2 4-tr cls, yo, pull through all lps on hook, rep from * around, ending last rep at **, join with sl st in beg st.

**Rnd 27:** Sl st in first ch sp, (3 sc, ch-4 picot, 3 sc, ch-4 picot, ch 5, sl st in 5th ch from hook, ch-4 picot, sl st in last st made, 3 sc, ch-4 picot, 3 sc) in same ch sp, *(3 sc, ch-4 picot, 3 sc) in next ch-7 sp, (2 sc, ch-4 picot, 2 sc) in each of next 9 ch-5 sps, (3 sc, ch-4 picot, 3 sc) in next ch-7 sp**, (3 sc, ch-4 picot, 3 sc, ch-4 picot, ch 5, sl st in 5th ch from hook, ch-4 picot, sl st in last st made, 3 sc, ch-4 picot, 3 sc) in next ch sp, rep from * around, ending last rep at **, join with sl st in beg sc. Fasten off. ■

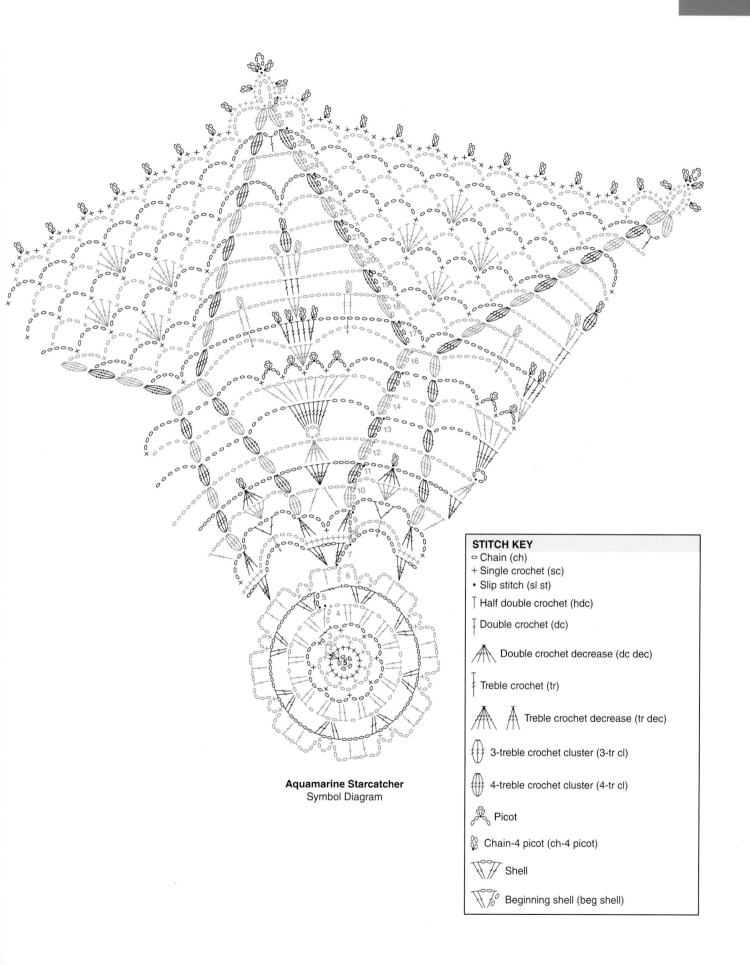

**Aquamarine Starcatcher**
Symbol Diagram

**STITCH KEY**

○ Chain (ch)

+ Single crochet (sc)

• Slip stitch (sl st)

┬ Half double crochet (hdc)

╎ Double crochet (dc)

⋀ Double crochet decrease (dc dec)

╎ Treble crochet (tr)

⋀ Treble crochet decrease (tr dec)

⬯ 3-treble crochet cluster (3-tr cl)

⬯ 4-treble crochet cluster (4-tr cl)

⚘ Picot

⚘ Chain-4 picot (ch-4 picot)

⋁ Shell

⋁ Beginning shell (beg shell)

# Golden
## Pineapples

DESIGN BY
**JUDY TEAGUE TREECE**

## SKILL LEVEL

**INTERMEDIATE**

## FINISHED SIZE
15½ inches in diameter

## MATERIALS
- DMC Cebelia size 10 crochet cotton (1¾ oz/284 yds/50g per ball): 2 balls #743 medium yellow
- Size 7/1.65mm steel crochet hook or size needed to obtain gauge

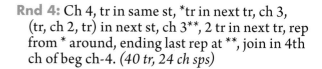

## GAUGE
4 dc = ½ inch; 5 dc rows = 1 inch

## PATTERN NOTES
Join with slip stitch as indicated unless otherwise stated.

Chain-4 at beginning of round counts as first treble crochet unless otherwise stated.

## DOILY
**Rnd 1:** Ch 6, **join** (see Pattern Notes) in beg ch to form ring, **ch 4** (see Pattern Notes), tr in ring, ch 2, [2 tr in ring, ch 2] 7 times, join in 4th of beg ch-4. (16 tr, 8 ch sps)

**Rnd 2:** Ch 4, tr in next tr, ch 2, tr in next ch-2 sp, ch 2, [tr in each of next 2 tr, ch 2, tr in next ch-2 sp, ch 2] around, join in 4th ch of beg ch-4. (24 tr, 16 ch sps)

**Rnd 3:** Ch 4, tr in next tr, ch 3, tr in next tr, ch 3, [tr in each of next 2 tr, ch 3, tr in next tr, ch 3] around, join in 4th ch of beg ch-4.

**Rnd 4:** Ch 4, tr in same st, *tr in next tr, ch 3, (tr, ch 2, tr) in next st, ch 3**, 2 tr in next tr, rep from * around, ending last rep at **, join in 4th ch of beg ch-4. (40 tr, 24 ch sps)

**Rnd 5:** Ch 4, tr in same st, *tr in each of next 2 tr, ch 3, sk next ch sp, (tr, ch 2, tr) in next ch-2 sp, ch 3**, 2 tr in next tr, rep from * around, ending last rep at **, join in 4th ch of beg ch-4. (48 tr, 24 ch sps)

**Rnd 6:** Ch 4, tr in same st, *tr in each of next 3 tr, ch 3, 7 tr in next ch-2 sp, ch 3**, 2 tr in next tr, rep from * around, ending last rep at **, join in 4th ch of beg ch-4. (96 tr, 16 ch sps)

**Rnd 7:** Ch 4, tr in same st, *tr in each of next 4 tr, ch 3, tr in next tr, [ch 1, tr in next tr] 6 times, ch 3**, 2 tr in next tr, rep from * around, ending last rep at **, join in 4th ch of beg ch-4. (104 tr, 48 ch-1 sps, 16 ch-3 sps)

**Rnd 8:** Ch 4, tr in same st, *tr in each of next 5 tr, ch 3, sc in next ch-1 sp, [ch 2, sc in next ch-1 sp] 5 times, ch 3**, 2 tr in next tr, rep from * around, ending last rep at **, join in 4th ch of beg ch-4. (56 tr, 48 sc, 40 ch-2 sps, 16 ch-3 sps)

**Rnd 9:** Ch 4, tr in each of next 2 tr, *ch 1, sk next tr, tr in each of next 3 tr, ch 4, sc in next ch-2 sp, [ch 2, sc in next ch-2 sp] 4 times, ch 4**, tr in each of next 3 tr, rep from * around, ending last rep at **, join in 4th ch of beg ch-4. (48 tr, 32 ch-2 sps, 16 ch-4 sps, 8 ch-1 sps)

**Rnd 10:** Ch 4, tr in each of next 2 tr, *ch 2, tr in each of next 3 tr, ch 4, sc in next ch-4 sp, ch 4, sc in next ch-2 sp, [ch 2, sc in next ch-2 sp] 3 times, ch 4, sc in next ch-4 sp, ch 4**, tr in each of next 3 tr, rep from * around, ending last rep at **, join in 4th ch of beg ch-4. *(48 tr, 32 ch-2 sps, 32 ch-4 sps)*

**Rnd 11:** Ch 4, tr in each of next 2 tr, *ch 3, tr in each of next 3 tr, ch 4, sc in next ch-4 sp, ch 6, sk next ch-4 sp, sc in next ch-2 sp, [ch 2, sc in next ch-2 sp] twice, ch 6, sk next ch-4 sp, sc in next ch-4 sp, ch 4**, tr in each of next 3 tr, rep from * around, ending last rep at **, join in 4th ch of beg ch-4. *(48 tr, 16 ch-2 sps, 16 ch-6 sps, 16 ch-4 sps, 8 ch-3 sps)*

**Rnd 12:** Ch 4, tr in each of next 2 tr, *ch 4, tr in each of next 3 tr, ch 4, sc in next ch-4 sp, ch 7, sk next ch-6 sp, sc in next ch-2 sp, ch 2, sc in next ch-2 sp, ch 7, sk next ch-6 sp, sc in next ch-4 sp, ch 4**, tr in each of next 3 tr, rep from * around, ending last rep at **, join in 4th ch of beg ch-4. *(48 tr, 24 ch-4 sps, 16 ch-7 sps, 8 ch-2 sps)*

**Rnd 13:** Ch 4, tr in each of next 2 tr, *ch 5, tr in each of next 3 tr, ch 4, sc in next ch-4 sp, ch 8, sk next ch-7 sp, sc in next ch-2 sp, ch 8, sk next ch-7 sp, sc in next ch-4 sp, ch 4**, tr in each of next 3 tr, rep from * around, ending last rep at **, join in 4th ch of beg ch-4. *(48 tr, 16 ch-8 sps, 16 ch-4 sps, 8 ch-5 sps)*

**Rnd 14:** Ch 4, tr in each of next 2 tr, *ch 5, sc in next ch-5 sp, ch 5, tr in each of next 3 tr, ch 4, sc in next ch-4 sp, [ch 6, sc in next ch sp] 3 times, ch 4**, tr in each of next 3 tr, rep from * around, ending last rep at **, join in 4th ch of beg ch-4. (48 tr, 24 ch-6 sps, 16 ch-5 sps, 16 ch-4 sps)

**Rnd 15:** Ch 4, tr in each of next 2 tr, *ch 5, sc in next ch-5 sp, ch 3, sc in next ch-5 sp, ch 5, tr in each of next 3 tr, ch 4, sc in next ch-4 sp, ch 5, sk next ch-6 sp, (sc, ch 5, sc) in next ch-6 sp, ch 5, sk next ch-6 sp, sc in next ch-4 sp, ch 4**, tr in each of next 3 tr, rep from * around, ending last rep at **, join in 4th ch of beg ch-4. (48 tr, 45 ch-5 sps, 16 ch-4 sps, 8 ch-3 sps)

**Rnd 16:** Ch 4, tr in same st, *2 tr in each of next 2 tr, ch 6, sk next ch-5 sp, sc in next ch-3 sp, ch 6, sk next ch-5 sp, 2 tr in each of next 3 tr, ch 4, sc in next ch-4 sp, ch 6, sk next ch sp, 7 tr in next ch sp, ch 6, sk next ch sp, sc in next ch-4 sp, ch 4**, 2 tr in next tr, rep from * around, ending last rep at **, join in 4th ch of beg ch-4. (152 tr, 32 ch-6 sps, 16 ch-4 sps)

**Rnd 17:** Ch 4, tr in each of next 5 tr, *ch 5, sc in next ch sp, ch 3, sc in next ch sp, ch 5, tr in each of next 6 tr, ch 4, sc in next ch-4 sp, ch 6, tr in next tr, [ch 1, tr in next tr] 6 times, ch 6, sk next ch sp, sc in next ch-4 sp, ch 4**, tr in each of next 6 tr, rep from * around, ending last rep at **, join in 4th ch of beg ch-4. (152 tr, 48 ch-1 sps, 16 ch-6 sps, 16 ch-5 sps, 16 ch-4 sps, 8 ch-3 sps)

**Rnd 18:** Ch 4, tr in each of next 5 tr, *ch 6, sk next ch sp, sc in next ch-3 sp, ch 6, sk next ch sp, tr in each of next 6 tr, ch 4, sc in next ch-4 sp, ch 6, sk next ch sp, sc in next ch-1 sp, [ch 2, sc in next ch-1 sp] 5 times, ch 6, sk next ch sp, sc in next ch-4 sp, ch 4**, tr in each of next 6 tr, rep from * around, ending last rep at **, join in 4th ch of beg ch-4. (96 tr, 40 ch-2 sps, 16 ch-6 sps, 16 ch-5 sps, 16 ch-4 sps)

**Rnd 19:** Ch 4, tr in each of next 5 tr, *ch 5, sc in next ch sp, ch 3, sc in next ch sp, ch 5, tr in each of next 6 tr, ch 5, sc in next ch-4 sp, ch 6, sk next ch sp, sc in next ch-2 sp, [ch 2, sc in next ch-2 sp] 4 times, ch 6, sk next ch sp, sc in next ch-4 sp, ch 5**, tr in each of next 6 tr, rep from * around, ending last rep at **, join in 4th ch of beg ch-4. (96 tr, 32 ch-2 sps, 32 ch-5 sps, 16 ch-6 sps, 8 ch-3 sps)

**Rnd 20:** Ch 4, tr in each of next 5 tr, *ch 6, sk next ch sp, sc in next ch-3 sp, ch 6, sk next ch sp, tr in each of next 6 tr, ch 5, sc in next ch-5 sp, ch 7, sk next ch sp, sc in next ch-2 sp, [ch 2, sc in next ch-2 sp] 3 times, ch 7, sk next ch sp, sc in next ch-5 sp, ch 5**, tr in each of next 6 tr, rep from * around, ending last rep at **, join in 4th ch of beg ch-4. (96 tr, 24 ch-2 sps, 16 ch-6 sps, 16 ch-5 sps, 16 ch-7 sps)

**Rnd 21:** Ch 4, tr in each of next 5 tr, *ch 5, sc in next ch sp, ch 3, sc in next ch sp, ch 5, tr in each of next 6 tr, ch 5, sc in next ch-5 sp, ch 8, sk next ch sp, sc in next ch-2 sp, [ch 2, sc in next ch-2 sp] twice, ch 8, sk next ch sp, sc in next ch-5 sp, ch 5**, tr in each of next 6 tr, rep from * around, ending last rep at **, join in 4th ch of beg ch-4. (96 tr, 32 ch-5 sps, 16 ch-8 sps, 16 ch-2 sps)

**Rnd 22:** Ch 4, tr in each of next 5 tr, *ch 6, sk next ch sp, sc in next ch-3 sp, ch 6, sk next ch sp, tr in each of next 6 tr, ch 5, sc in next ch-5 sp, ch 10, sk next ch sp, sc in next ch-2 sp, ch 2, sc in next ch-2 sp, ch 10, sk next ch sp, sc in next ch-5 sp, ch 5**, tr in each of next 6 tr, rep from * around, ending last rep at **, join in 4th ch of beg ch-4. (96 tr, 16 ch-6 sps, 16 ch-9 sps, 16 ch-5 sps, 8 ch-2 sps)

**Rnd 23:** Ch 4, tr in each of next 5 tr, *ch 6, sc in next ch sp, ch 5, sc in next ch sp, ch 6, tr in each of next 6 tr, ch 5, sc in next ch sp, ch 10, sk next ch sp, sc in next ch-2 sp, ch 10, sk next ch sp, sc in next ch sp, ch 5**, tr in each of next 6 tr, rep from * around, ending last rep at **, join in 4th ch of beg ch-4. (96 tr, 24 ch-5 sps, 16 ch-6 sps, 16 ch-10 sps)

**Rnd 24:** Ch 4, tr in each of next 5 tr, *[ch 5, sc in next ch sp] 3 times, ch 5, tr in each of next 6 tr, [ch 5, sc in next ch sp] 4 times, ch 5**, tr in each of next 6 tr, rep from * around, ending last rep at **, join in 4th ch of beg ch-4. (96 tr, 72 ch-5 sps)

**Rnd 25:** Ch 1, sc in each tr and 6 sc in each ch sp around, join in beg sc. (528 sc)

**Rnd 26:** Ch 1, sc in first st, ch 4, sl st in top of last sc made, ch 4, sk next 3 sts, [sc in next st, ch 4, sl st in top of last sc made, ch 4, sk next 3 sts] around, join in beg sc. Fasten off. ■

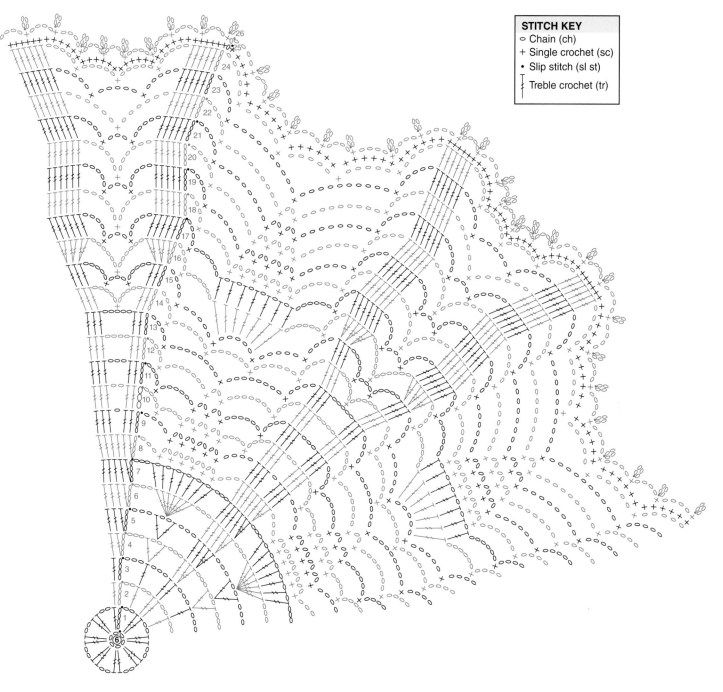

**STITCH KEY**
- ○ Chain (ch)
- + Single crochet (sc)
- • Slip stitch (sl st)
- Treble crochet (tr)

**Golden Pineapples**
Symbol Diagram

# Antique Pineapple & Cones

DESIGN BY
**JUDY TEAGUE TREECE**

## SKILL LEVEL

**INTERMEDIATE**

## FINISHED SIZE

12¼ inches in diameter

## MATERIALS

- DMC Cebelia size 10 crochet cotton (1¾ oz/284 yds/50g per ball): 2 balls #842 coffee cream
- Size 7/1.65mm steel crochet hook or size needed to obtain gauge

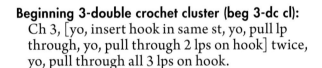

## GAUGE

4 dc = ½ inch; 5 dc rows = 1 inch

## PATTERN NOTES

Join with slip stitch as indicated unless otherwise stated.

Chain-3 at beginning of round counts as first double crochet unless otherwise stated.

## SPECIAL STITCHES

**Beginning cluster (beg cl):** Ch 3, yo, insert hook in next ch sp, yo, pull lp through, yo, pull through 2 lps on hook, yo, insert hook in same ch sp, yo, pull lp through, yo, pull through 2 lps on hook, yo, insert hook in next st, yo, pull lp through, yo, pull through 2 lps on hook, yo, pull through all 4 lps on hook.

**Cluster (cl):** Yo, insert hook in next st, yo, pull lp through, yo, pull through 2 lps on hook, yo, insert hook in next ch sp, yo, pull lp through, yo, pull through 2 lps on hook, yo, insert hook in same ch sp, yo, pull lp through, yo, pull through 2 lps on hook, yo, insert hook in next st, yo, pull lp through, yo, pull through 2 lps on hook, yo, pull through all 5 lps on hook.

**Beginning 3-double crochet cluster (beg 3-dc cl):** Ch 3, [yo, insert hook in same st, yo, pull lp through, yo, pull through 2 lps on hook] twice, yo, pull through all 3 lps on hook.

**3-double crochet cluster (3-dc cl):** Yo, insert hook in next st, yo, pull lp through, yo, pull through 2 lps on hook, [yo, insert hook in same st, yo, pull lp through, yo, pull through 2 lps on hook] twice, yo, pull through all 4 lps on hook.

## DOILY

**Rnd 1:** Ch 6, **join** (see Pattern Notes) in beg ch to form ring, **ch 3** (see Pattern Notes), 20 dc in ring, join in 3rd ch of beg ch-3. (21 dc)

**Rnd 2:** Ch 3, dc in next st, ch 3, sk next st, [dc in each of next 2 sts, ch 3, sk next st] around, join in 3rd ch of beg ch-3. (14 dc, 7 ch sps)

**Rnd 3:** Ch 3, dc in same st, dc in next st, ch 3, sk next ch sp, [2 dc in next st, dc in next st, ch 3, sk next ch sp] around, join in 3rd ch of beg ch-3. (21 dc, 7 ch sps)

**Rnd 4:** Ch 3, dc in same st, dc in each of next 2 sts, ch 3, sk next ch sp, [2 dc in next st, dc in each of next 2 sts, ch 3, sk next ch sp] around, join in 3rd ch of beg ch-3. (28 dc, 7 ch sps)

**Rnd 5:** Ch 3, dc in same st, dc in each of next 3 sts, ch 4, sk next ch sp, [2 dc in next st, dc in each of next 3 sts, ch 4, sk next ch sp] around, join in 3rd ch of beg ch-3. (35 dc, 7 ch sps)

**Rnd 6:** Ch 3, dc in same st, dc in each of next 4 sts, ch 5, sk next ch sp, [2 dc in next st, dc in each of next 4 sts, ch 5, sk next ch sp] around, join in 3rd ch of beg ch-3. (42 dc, 7 ch sps)

**Rnd 7:** Ch 3, dc in each of next 5 sts, ch 6, sk next ch sp, [dc in each of next 6 sts, ch 6, sk next ch sp] around, join in 3rd ch of beg ch-3.

**Rnd 8:** Ch 3, dc in each of next 5 sts, ch 7, sk next ch sp, [dc in each of next 6 sts, ch 7, sk next ch sp] around, join in 3rd ch of beg ch-3.

**Rnd 9:** Ch 3, dc in each of next 5 sts, ch 4, sc in next ch sp, ch 4, [dc in each of next 6 sts, ch 4, sc in next ch sp, ch 4] around, join in 3rd ch of beg ch-3. *(42 dc, 14 ch sps, 7 sc)*

**Rnd 10:** Ch 3, dc in each of next 2 sts, *ch 2, dc in each of next 3 sts, ch 4, sc in next ch sp, ch 3, sc in next ch sp, ch 4**, dc in each of next 3 sts, rep from * around, ending last rep at **, join in 3rd ch of beg ch-3. *(42 dc, 14 ch-4 sps, 14 sc, 7 ch-2 sps, 7 ch-3 sps)*

**Rnd 11:** Ch 3, dc in each of next 2 sts, *ch 2, sk next ch sp, dc in each of next 3 sts, ch 4, sc in next ch sp, ch 2, (dc, ch 1, dc) in next ch sp, ch 2, sc in next ch sp, ch 4**, dc in each of next 3 sts, rep from * around, ending last rep at **, join in 3rd ch of beg ch-3. *(56 dc, 21 ch-2 sps, 14 ch-4 sps, 14 sc, 7 ch-1 sps)*

**Rnd 12:** Ch 3, dc in each of next 2 sts, *ch 2, sk next ch sp, dc in each of next 3 sts, ch 4, sc in next ch sp, ch 4, sk next ch sp, (dc, ch 2, dc) in next ch-1 sp, ch 4, sk next ch sp, sc in next ch sp, ch 4**, dc in each of next 3 sts, rep from * around, ending last rep at **, join in 3rd ch of beg ch-3. *(56 dc, 28 ch-4 sps, 14 ch-2 sps, 14 sc)*

**Rnd 13:** Ch 3, *2 dc in next st, dc in next st, ch 2, sk next ch sp, dc in next st, 2 dc in next st, dc in next st, ch 4, sc in next ch sp, ch 4, sk next ch sp, (dc, [ch 1, dc] twice) in next ch-2 sp, ch 4, sk next ch sp, sc in next ch sp, ch 4**, dc in next st, rep from * around, ending last rep at **, join in 3rd ch of beg ch-3. *(77 dc, 28 ch-4 sps, 14 ch-1 sps, 14 sc, 7 ch-2 sps)*

**Rnd 14:** Ch 3, dc in each of next 3 sts, *ch 2, sk next ch sp, dc in each of next 4 sts, ch 4, sc in next ch sp, ch 4, sk next ch sp, (dc, ch 1, dc) in next ch sp, ch 1, (dc, ch 1, dc) in next ch sp, ch 4, sk next ch sp, sc in next ch sp, ch 4**, dc in each of next 4 sts, rep from * around, ending last rep at **, join in 3rd ch of beg ch-3. *(84 dc, 28 ch-4 sps, 21 ch-1 sps, 14 sc, 7 ch-2 sps)*

**Rnd 15:** Ch 3, dc in next st, ***dc dec** *(see Stitch Guide)* in next 2 sts, ch 2, sk next ch sp, dc dec in next 2 sts, dc in each of next 2 sts, ch 4, sc in next ch sp, ch 5, sk next ch sp, (dc, ch 1, dc) in each of next 3 ch-1 sps, ch 5, sk next ch sp, sc in next ch sp, ch 4**, dc in each of next 2 sts, rep from * around, ending last rep at **, join in 3rd ch of beg ch-3. *(84 dc, 21 ch-1 sps, 14 ch-4 sps, 14 ch-5 sps, 14 sc, 7 ch-2 sps)*

**Rnd 16:** Ch 3, *dc dec in next 2 sts, ch 2, sk next ch sp, dc dec in next 2 sts, dc in next st, ch 4, sc in next ch sp, ch 5, sk next ch sp, (dc, ch 1, dc, ch 2) in each of next 2 ch-1 sps, (dc, ch 1, dc) in next ch sp, ch 5, sk next ch-5 sp, sc in next ch sp, ch 4**, dc in next st, rep from * around, ending last rep at **, join in 3rd ch of beg ch-3. *(70 dc, 21 ch-1 sps, 21 ch-2 sps, 14 ch-5 sps, 14 ch-4 sps, 14 sc)*

**Rnd 17:** Ch 3 *(counted as a st)*, dc in next st, *ch 2, sk next ch sp, dc dec in next 2 sts, ch 4, sc in next ch sp, ch 5, sk next ch sp, (dc, ch 1, dc) in next ch-1 sp, ch 3, sk next ch-2 sp, (sc, ch 6, sc) in next ch-1 sp, ch 3, sk next ch-2 sp, (dc, ch 1, dc) in next ch-1 sp, ch 5, sk next ch sp, sc in next ch sp, ch 4**, dc dec in next 2 sts, rep from * around, ending last rep at**, join in top of beg dc. *(56 dc, 21 ch-2 sps, 14 ch-6 sps, 14 ch-4 sps, 14 sc, 7 ch-6 sps)*

**Rnd 18: Beg cl** *(see Special Stitches)*, *ch 4, sc in next ch sp, ch 8, sk next ch sp, (dc, ch 1, dc) in next ch-1 sp, ch 2, 9 dc in next ch-6 sp, ch 2, sk next ch-2 sp, (dc, ch 1, dc) in next ch-1 sp, ch 8, sk next ch sp, sc in next ch sp, ch 4**, **cl** *(see Special Stitches)*, rep from * around, ending last rep at **, join in top of beg cl. *(91 dc, 7 cls)*

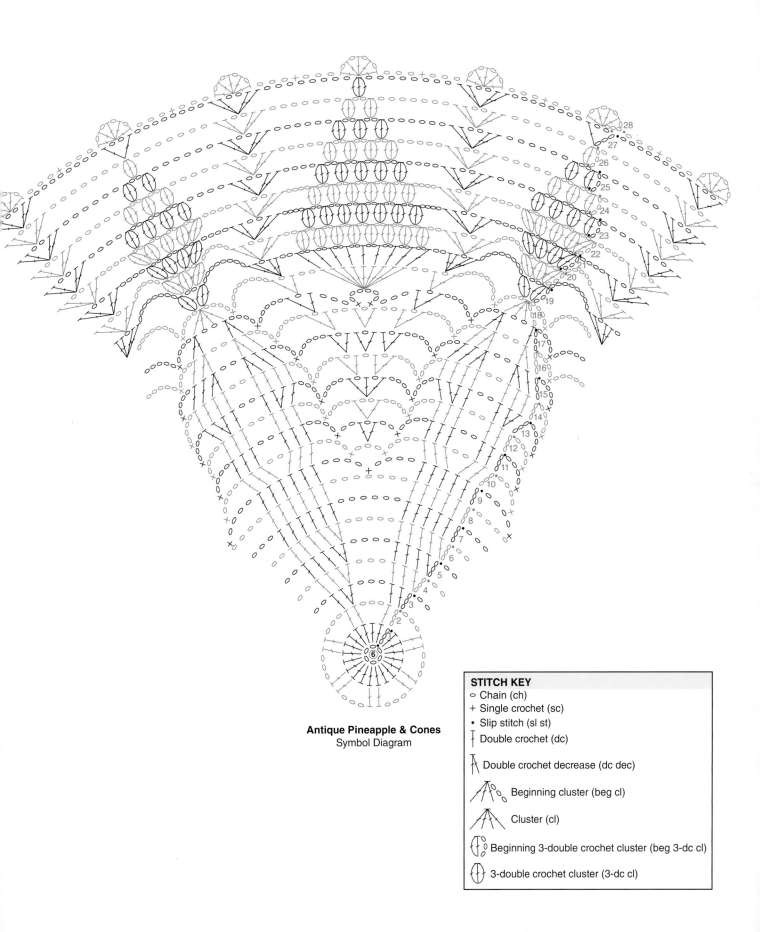

**Antique Pineapple & Cones**
Symbol Diagram

**STITCH KEY**

- ⌒ Chain (ch)
- + Single crochet (sc)
- • Slip stitch (sl st)
- † Double crochet (dc)
- ⋀ Double crochet decrease (dc dec)
- Beginning cluster (beg cl)
- Cluster (cl)
- Beginning 3-double crochet cluster (beg 3-dc cl)
- 3-double crochet cluster (3-dc cl)

**Rnd 19:** (**Beg 3-dc cl**—*see Special Stitches*, ch 2, **3-dc cl**—*see Special Stitches*) in first st, *ch 8, sk next 2 ch sps, (2 dc, ch 1, 2 dc) in next ch-1 sp, ch 2, [dc in next st, ch 2] 9 times, sk next ch sp, (2 dc, ch 2, 2 dc) in next ch-1 sp, ch 8, sk next 2 ch sps**, (3-dc cl, ch 2, 3-dc cl) in next cl, rep from * around, ending last rep at **, join in top of beg cl. (*119 dc, 14 cls*)

**Rnd 20:** (Sl st, beg 3-dc cl, [ch 2, 3-dc cl] twice) in first ch sp, *ch 5, sk next ch sp, (2 dc, ch 2, 2 dc) in next ch-1 sp, ch 2, sk next ch sp, [3-dc cl in next ch-2 sp, ch 2] 8 times, sk next ch sp, (2 dc, ch 2, 2 dc) in next ch-1 sp, ch 5, sk next ch sp**, (3-dc cl, [ch 2, 3-dc cl] twice) in next ch sp, rep from * around, ending last rep at **, join in top of beg cl. (*77 cls, 56 dc*)

**Rnd 21:** (Sl st, beg 3-dc cl, ch 2, 3-dc cl) in first ch sp, *ch 2, (3-dc cl, ch 2, 3-dc cl) in next ch sp, ch 4, sk next ch sp, (2 dc, ch 2, 2 dc) in next ch sp, ch 4, sk next ch sp, [3-dc cl in next ch sp, ch 2] 6 times, 3-dc cl in next ch sp, ch 4, sk next ch sp, (2 dc, ch 2, 2 dc) in next ch sp, ch 4, sk next ch sp**, (3-dc cl, ch 2, 3-dc cl) in next ch sp, rep from * around, ending last rep at **, join in top of beg cl.

**Rnd 22:** (Sl st, beg 3-dc cl, ch 2, 3-dc cl) in first ch sp, *ch 2, 3-dc cl in next ch sp, ch 2, (3-dc cl, ch 2, 3-dc cl) in next ch sp, ch 4, sk next ch sp, (2 dc, ch 2, 2 dc) in next ch sp, ch 4, sk next ch sp, [3-dc cl in next ch sp, ch 2] 5 times, 3-dc cl in next ch sp, ch 4, sk next ch sp, (2 dc, ch 2, 2 dc) in next ch sp, ch 4, sk next ch sp**, (3-dc cl, ch 2, 3-dc cl) in next ch sp, rep from * around, ending last rep at **, join in top of beg cl.

**Rnd 23:** (Sl st, beg 3-dc cl) in first ch sp, *[ch 2, 3-dc cl in next ch sp] 3 times, ch 4, sk next ch sp, (2 dc, ch 2, 2 dc) in next ch sp, ch 4, sk next ch sp, [3-dc cl in next ch sp, ch 2] 4 times, 3-dc cl in next ch sp, ch 4, sk next ch sp, (2 dc, ch 2, 2 dc) in next ch sp, ch 4, sk next ch sp**, 3-dc cl in next ch sp, rep from * around, ending last rep at **, join in top of beg cl. (*63 cls, 56 dc*)

**Rnd 24:** (Sl st, beg 3-dc cl) in first ch sp, *[ch 2, 3-dc cl in next ch sp] twice, ch 5, sk next ch sp, (2 dc, ch 2, 2 dc) in next ch sp, ch 5, sk next ch sp, [3-dc cl in next ch sp, ch 2] 3 times, 3-dc cl in next ch sp, ch 5, sk next ch sp, (2 dc, ch 2, 2 dc) in next ch sp, ch 5, sk next ch sp**, 3-dc cl in next ch sp, rep from * around, ending last rep at **, join in top of beg cl. (*56 dc, 49 cls*)

**Rnd 25:** (Sl st, beg 3-dc cl) in first ch sp, *ch 2, 3-dc cl in next ch sp, ch 6, sk next ch sp, (2 dc, ch 2, 2 dc) in next ch sp, ch 6, sk next ch sp, [3-dc cl in next ch sp, ch 2] twice, 3-dc cl in next ch sp, ch 6, sk next ch sp, (2 dc, ch 2, 2 dc) in next ch sp, ch 6, sk next ch sp**, 3-dc cl in next ch sp, rep from * around, ending last rep at **, join in top of beg cl. (*56 dc, 35 cls*)

**Rnd 26:** (Sl st, beg 3-dc cl) in first ch sp, *ch 7, sk next ch sp, (2 dc, ch 2, 2 dc) in next ch sp, ch 7, sk next ch sp, 3-dc cl in next ch sp, ch 2, 3-dc cl in next ch sp, ch 7, sk next ch sp, (2 dc, ch 2, 2 dc) in next ch sp, ch 7, sk next ch sp**, 3-dc cl in next ch sp, rep from * around, ending last rep at **, join in top of beg cl. (*56 dc, 21 cls*)

**Rnd 27:** Ch 5 (*counts as first dc and ch-2 sp*), dc in same st, *ch 8, sk next ch sp, (2 dc, ch 2, 2 dc) in next ch sp, ch 8, sk next ch sp, 3-dc cl in next ch sp, ch 8, sk next ch sp, (2 dc, ch 2, 2 dc) in next ch sp, ch 8, sk next ch sp**, (dc, ch 2, dc) in next cl, rep from * around, ending last rep at **, join in 3rd ch of beg ch-5. (*70 dc, 7 cls*)

**Rnd 28:** Sl st in first ch sp, ch 4 (*counts as first dc and ch-1 sp*), (dc, [ch 1, dc] 3 times) in same sp, *ch 3, sc in next ch sp, ch 3, (dc, [ch 1, dc] 4 times) in next ch-2 sp, ch 3, sc in next ch sp, ch 3, (dc, [ch 1, dc] 4 times) in next cl, ch 3, sc in next ch sp, ch 3, (dc, [ch 1, dc] 4 times) in next ch sp, ch 3, sc in next ch sp, ch 3**, (dc, [ch 1, dc] 4 times) in next ch-2 sp, rep from * around, ending last rep at **, join in 3rd ch of beg ch-4. Fasten off. ■

# STITCH GUIDE

## STITCH ABBREVIATIONS

| | |
|---|---|
| beg | begin/begins/beginning |
| bpdc | back post double crochet |
| bpsc | back post single crochet |
| bptr | back post treble crochet |
| CC | contrasting color |
| ch(s) | chain(s) |
| ch- | refers to chain or space previously made (i.e., ch-1 space) |
| ch sp(s) | chain space(s) |
| cl(s) | cluster(s) |
| cm | centimeter(s) |
| dc | double crochet (singular/plural) |
| dc dec | double crochet 2 or more stitches together, as indicated |
| dec | decrease/decreases/decreasing |
| dtr | double treble crochet |
| ext | extended |
| fpdc | front post double crochet |
| fpsc | front post single crochet |
| fptr | front post treble crochet |
| g | gram(s) |
| hdc | half double crochet |
| hdc dec | half double crochet 2 or more stitches together, as indicated |
| inc | increase/increases/increasing |
| lp(s) | loop(s) |
| MC | main color |
| mm | millimeter(s) |
| oz | ounce(s) |
| pc | popcorn(s) |
| rem | remain/remains/remaining |
| rep(s) | repeat(s) |
| rnd(s) | round(s) |
| RS | right side |
| sc | single crochet (singular/plural) |
| sc dec | single crochet 2 or more stitches together, as indicated |
| sk | skip/skipped/skipping |
| sl st(s) | slip stitch(es) |
| sp(s) | space(s)/spaced |
| st(s) | stitch(es) |
| tog | together |
| tr | treble crochet |
| trtr | triple treble |
| WS | wrong side |
| yd(s) | yard(s) |
| yo | yarn over |

### YARN CONVERSION

| OUNCES TO GRAMS | | GRAMS TO OUNCES | |
|---|---|---|---|
| 1 | 28.4 | 25 | 7/8 |
| 2 | 56.7 | 40 | 1 2/3 |
| 3 | 85.0 | 50 | 1 3/4 |
| 4 | 113.4 | 100 | 3 1/2 |

| UNITED STATES | | UNITED KINGDOM |
|---|---|---|
| sl st (slip stitch) | = | sc (single crochet) |
| sc (single crochet) | = | dc (double crochet) |
| hdc (half double crochet) | = | htr (half treble crochet) |
| dc (double crochet) | = | tr (treble crochet) |
| tr (treble crochet) | = | dtr (double treble crochet) |
| dtr (double treble crochet) | = | ttr (triple treble crochet) |
| skip | = | miss |

**Reverse single crochet (reverse sc):** Ch 1, sk first st, working from left to right, insert hook in next st from front to back, draw up lp on hook, yo and draw through both lps on hook.

**Chain (ch):** Yo, pull through lp on hook.

**Single crochet (sc):** Insert hook in st, yo, pull through st, yo, pull through both lps on hook.

**Double crochet (dc):** Yo, insert hook in st, yo, pull through st, [yo, pull through 2 lps] twice.

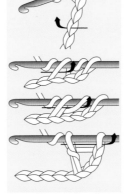

**Front loop (front lp) Back loop (back lp)**

Front Loop    Back Loop

**Front post stitch (fp): Back post stitch (bp):** When working post st, insert hook from right to left around post of st on previous row.

Back    Front

Post of Stitch

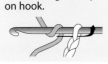

**Half double crochet (hdc):** Yo, insert hook in st, yo, pull through st, yo, pull through all 3 lps on hook.

**Double treble crochet (dtr):** Yo 3 times, insert hook in st, yo, pull through st, [yo, pull through 2 lps] 4 times.

**Slip stitch (sl st):** Insert hook in st, pull through both lps on hook.

**Chain color change (ch color change)** Yo with new color, draw through last lp on hook.

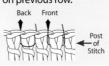

**Double crochet color change (dc color change)** Drop first color, yo with new color, draw through last 2 lps of st.

**Treble crochet (tr):** Yo twice, insert hook in st, yo, pull through st, [yo, pull through 2 lps] 3 times.

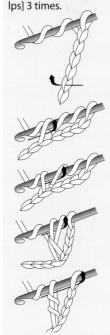

**Single crochet decrease (sc dec):** (Insert hook, yo, draw lp through) in each of the sts indicated, yo, draw through all lps on hook.

Example of 2-sc dec

**Half double crochet decrease (hdc dec):** (Yo, insert hook, yo, draw lp through) in each of the sts indicated, yo, draw through all lps on hook.

Example of 2-hdc dec

**Double crochet decrease (dc dec):** (Yo, insert hook, yo, draw lp through, yo, draw through 2 lps on hook) in each of the sts indicated, yo, draw through all lps on hook.

Example of 2-dc dec

**Treble crochet decrease (tr dec):** Holding back last lp of each st, tr in each of the sts indicated, yo, pull through all lps on hook.

Example of 2-tr dec

# Metric
## Conversion
## Charts

### METRIC CONVERSIONS

| | | | | |
|---|---|---|---|---|
| yards | x | .9144 | = | metres (m) |
| yards | x | 91.44 | = | centimetres (cm) |
| inches | x | 2.54 | = | centimetres (cm) |
| inches | x | 25.40 | = | millimetres (mm) |
| inches | x | .0254 | = | metres (m) |

| | | | | |
|---|---|---|---|---|
| centimetres | x | .3937 | = | inches |
| metres | x | 1.0936 | = | yards |

### INCHES INTO MILLIMETRES & CENTIMETRES (Rounded off slightly)

| inches | mm | cm | inches | cm | inches | cm | inches | cm |
|---|---|---|---|---|---|---|---|---|
| 1/8 | 3 | 0.3 | 5 | 12.5 | 21 | 53.5 | 38 | 96.5 |
| 1/4 | 6 | 0.6 | 5 1/2 | 14 | 22 | 56 | 39 | 99 |
| 3/8 | 10 | 1 | 6 | 15 | 23 | 58.5 | 40 | 101.5 |
| 1/2 | 13 | 1.3 | 7 | 18 | 24 | 61 | 41 | 104 |
| 5/8 | 15 | 1.5 | 8 | 20.5 | 25 | 63.5 | 42 | 106.5 |
| 3/4 | 20 | 2 | 9 | 23 | 26 | 66 | 43 | 109 |
| 7/8 | 22 | 2.2 | 10 | 25.5 | 27 | 68.5 | 44 | 112 |
| 1 | 25 | 2.5 | 11 | 28 | 28 | 71 | 45 | 114.5 |
| 1 1/4 | 32 | 3.2 | 12 | 30.5 | 29 | 73.5 | 46 | 117 |
| 1 1/2 | 38 | 3.8 | 13 | 33 | 30 | 76 | 47 | 119.5 |
| 1 3/4 | 45 | 4.5 | 14 | 35.5 | 31 | 79 | 48 | 122 |
| 2 | 50 | 5 | 15 | 38 | 32 | 81.5 | 49 | 124.5 |
| 2 1/2 | 65 | 6.5 | 16 | 40.5 | 33 | 84 | 50 | 127 |
| 3 | 75 | 7.5 | 17 | 43 | 34 | 86.5 | | |
| 3 1/2 | 90 | 9 | 18 | 46 | 35 | 89 | | |
| 4 | 100 | 10 | 19 | 48.5 | 36 | 91.5 | | |
| 4 1/2 | 115 | 11.5 | 20 | 51 | 37 | 94 | | |

### KNITTING NEEDLES CONVERSION CHART

| Canada/U.S. | 0 | 1 | 2 | 3 | 4 | 5 | 6 | 7 | 8 | 9 | 10 | 10½ | 11 | 13 | 15 |
|---|---|---|---|---|---|---|---|---|---|---|---|---|---|---|---|
| Metric (mm) | 2 | 2¼ | 2¾ | 3¼ | 3½ | 3¾ | 4 | 4½ | 5 | 5½ | 6 | 6½ | 8 | 9 | 10 |

### CROCHET HOOKS CONVERSION CHART

| Canada/U.S. | 1/B | 2/C | 3/D | 4/E | 5/F | 6/G | 8/H | 9/I | 10/J | 10½/K | N |
|---|---|---|---|---|---|---|---|---|---|---|---|
| Metric (mm) | 2.25 | 2.75 | 3.25 | 3.5 | 3.75 | 4.25 | 5 | 5.5 | 6 | 6.5 | 9.0 |

*Annie's*

*Doilies With Symbol Crochet* is published by Annie's, 306 East Parr Road, Berne, IN 46711. Printed in USA. Copyright © 2012, 2017 Annie's. All rights reserved. This publication may not be reproduced in part or in whole without written permission from the publisher.

**RETAIL STORES:** If you would like to carry this pattern book or any other Annie's publications, visit AnniesWSL.com.

Every effort has been made to ensure that the instructions in this pattern book are complete and accurate. We cannot, however, take responsibility for human error, typographical mistakes or variations in individual work. Please visit AnniesCustomerService.com to check for pattern updates.

ISBN: 978-1-59635-745-7
13 14 15 16 17